CAMPAIGNS
AND HOW TO WIN THEM!

Clare Watson brings a decade of experience of developing campaigns and projects to this book. She has been involved with a number of AIDS education initiatives and environmental groups, including The Irish Quilt four 1991 and Greenpeace. More recently, she co-ordinated the Dun Laoghaire Harbour Action Group campaign, and the 'No To Incineration' campaign in Sandymount/Ringsend. **Mícheál Ó Cadhla** has worked with Greenpeace for four years, both on land and sea. He is currently co-ordinating the efforts of voluntary groups campaigning on environment, development, conservation and human rights in his home town, Waterford. **Cristíona Ní Dhurcáin** has spent four years working on Greenpeace campaigns, both in the Irish office and at sea, and has also worked with Trócaire. All three are involved in the setting up of Ecolink – an organisation which aims to provide support and networking services to people working on environmental and sustainable development issues.

CAMPAIGNS

AND HOW TO WIN THEM!

Clare Watson,
Mícheál Ó Cadhla
Cristíona Ní Dhurcáin,

WOLFHOUND PRESS

First published 1997 by
WOLFHOUND PRESS Ltd
68 Mountjoy Square
Dublin 1

British Library Cataloguing in Publication Data
A catalogue record for this book is available from the British Library.

The authors' share of profits from this book go to Ecolink.

ISBN 0 86327 554 0

PICTURE CREDITS
(Page 1) Top: courtesy of Marc O'Sullivan. Bottom © Derek Speirs/Report
(Page 2) Top: © Greenpeace/Sea Byrne.
(Page 3) Top: © The *Irish Times*. Bottom: courtesy of Marc O'Sullivan.
(Page 4) Top: By kind permission of Amnesty International. Bottom: photograph by
Kim Haughton.
(Page 5) Top: By kind permission of Martin Hannigan. Bottom: © Derek Speirs.
(Page 6) Top: courtesy of A. Gough. By kind permission of the Red Ribbon Project.
Bottom: courtesy of CIL.
(Page 7) Top: © Derek Speirs/Report. Bottom: With kind permission of CIWF.
© Marc O'Sullivan.
(Page 8) Top: © Derek Speirs. By kind permission of the East Timor Campaign.
Bottom: courtesy of *Irish Independent*.

TEXT CREDIT
The authors wish to acknowledge the *IPA Administration Yearbook and Diary* as
source material for Appendix A.

Printed on recycled paper
Typesetting: Wolfhound Press
Cover design and illustration: Ed Miliano
Printed and bound by The Guernsey Press Co. Ltd, Guersney, Channel Islands

CONTENTS

FOREWORD

I wish I had had this book eighteen years ago, when I was starting out as a campaigner for Irish CND, devising a Peace Education programme for the country's schools! This campaigners' handbook would also have proved invaluable to me in establishing the 'Chernobyl Children's Project', the charity that I founded in 1991 to help ease the suffering of the children affected by the world's worst nuclear disaster. As it was, we had to learn the hard way – through experience – in order to devise these guidelines and to put these systems into place to run both Irish CND and the Project as effectively as possible. I cannot stress enough how much time and energy you will save by following the steps to successful campaigning that are outlined here. You will also find this book a real pleasure to read: the style is totally *jargon-free* and exceptionally clear and accessible.

The practical advice that the authors have provided cannot be faulted – this is certainly not a guide for those who want to talk about action – it is for people who want to get things done! The sections on the resources you will need, drawing up a budget, fund-raising, office administration, and good decision-making and structures are all excellent and very well-explained. Without the hard *nitty-gritty* day to day working procedures in place the most inspired ideas will not translate into reality. I would certainly subscribe to the need for clear and understood guidelines to be laid down in working practices in order to ensure that the many different kinds of people involved in your campaign or organisation all know that the same rules apply to everyone – this is a good way to avoid 'egos' from becoming more important than your common goals. I was also pleased to note the tribute paid to the energy and enthusiasm of young people, in Chapter 5 on fund-raising: this made me think of two of the Project's best fund-raisers and office volunteers: Janice Lennon age 13 and Maria Dorgan age 12, who are certainly an inspiration to the office staff here.

The writers identify the elements that will be crucial to the success of your campaign: an action plan, strategy, aims and vision. I like the way in which the 'fun part' of any efforts to bring about change is highlighted in the action plan section, and also agree with the comment that while plans are important you will need to be flexible – certainly there have been many times when my work plan has altered several times in the course of a day as events have necessitated reassessing and changing priorities! When children need treatment or a medical aid convoy is being sent out from Ireland to Belarus, then it has been the combination of keeping in mind all that needs to be done, and being able to be flexible that has produced results. Strategy is very well described here as *'the skeleton around which you will build your campaign, fleshing it out with tactics'*, and all the differing options appropriate to different types of campaigns are very clearly laid out for you. Identifying long and short-term aims and 'attainable goals' is very important. You need to give yourself the opportunity to build on your first successes. That will give you the confidence to make progress. I am sometimes amazed at the way in which the 'Chernobyl Children's Project' has grown from small beginnings when we brought thirty children to Cork in the summer of 1991 for rest and recuperation, to the visit of 1,200 children to Ireland, the UK and Boston USA in the summer of 1996!

Communication is a vital skill for any campaigner and I have never come across a better guide to finding and presenting information than this: I can certainly vouch for the value of the Internet both as a source of useful facts and as a means of promoting your work – the Project's web-site has generated interest and support from around the world. If you follow the suggestions on writing press releases, giving interviews and organising press conferences here you will be giving an impression of total professionalism. That means you will be taken seriously. Credibility is vital to a successful campaign, and that is why the run-down on sources of data here will be crucial to you. Every means of promoting your work is exhaustively covered and there is a very contemporary approach to the need for a positive message which I feel is much more attractive to the public than simply saying 'No'. The motto of the 'Chernobyl Children's Project' is 'Offering Hope to Live'.

This handbook is full of moving and inspiring reflections on what drives and motivates us to work for different goals and how best we can achieve them. Perhaps my favourite of these is the quotation by Yuri Gagarin: *'Looking at the Earth from afar you realise it is too small for conflict and just big enough for co-operation.'*

In my schools' work, I always encourage the children to look back and read the words of the first astronauts who went into space, and to try and share some of the magic those men experienced when they looked down on this big, blue, beautiful planet with no frontiers. This leads on to talking about the miracle of life on earth and how we could have been just another barren planet in the galaxy of the Milky Way, had it not been for the ozone layer which has wrapped us up and swathed us from the dangers of the ultra-violet rays of the sun. Describing how life was able to evolve over billions of years invariably gets a few gasps of excitement and the children are thrilled no end as they learn to discover the beauty of their home.

What informs any campaign is vision: all of us involved in working for a better future need to constantly keep in mind our vision of life on this planet as it could and should be, with the freedom for all of us to develop our full potential. It is not easy: knowing that old habits die hard makes me very aware of the difficult pathway ahead. But I think that in our willingness to protect the earth, the reward will be great, for our children will someday inherit the earth in all its mystery and wonder. Let that be so.

Adi Roche
Executive Director
Chernobyl Children's Project

ACKNOWLEDGEMENTS

To Mick Flynn for his patience, his time and his very welcome editing expertise...

To Adi Roche for her inspiring dedication to her cause and for writing the foreword...

To David Flynn and Stuart Margetson for all the work they put into the Legal and Planning chapter, and to Patricia McKenna, MEP for her assistance on the EU section of the Political Lobbying chapter...

To the authors of the anecdotes who helped to bring the book alive, and to all of those who helped us in our quest for photographs...

To the following for so generously reading and commenting on parts of the draft version – Mary-Anne Bartlett, Gerry Boland, Ann Carroll, Karina Carroll (Ireland On-Line), Derry Chambers, Michael Collins, Ciaran Cuffe, Mike Garvey, Laura George, Dermot Lacey, Kay Lynch, Christine Magee, Eleanor McClorey, Geraldine Murphy, Joan Murphy, Orla Ní Eili, Patrick Nolan, Mary Phelan, Eamonn Ryan, Moynagh Sullivan...

To all the great campaigners, far too many to name individually, who have worked tirelessly with us on various campaigns, and who, through their persistence, good humour and willingnes to do just about anything, made sure that many contests were won and a lot of fun was had along the way...

And in particular to Fran Power, who gave us the initial encouragement to put this handbook together, and to Ulf Birgander, David Enever, Alan & Gráinne Foreman, Charly Juchler, Albert Kuiken, Arthur Leahy, Aodh MacGrianna, Margareta McKenna, Rachel Martin, Grace & Emer O'Sullivan, Massimo Tixi, David Whelan, for their invaluable support, inspiration and guidance over the years...

To our friends and families for continuing to put up with us and our sometimes unorthodox and uexpected antics, and for being around to lend an ear and often a lot more...

A VERY GRATEFUL THANK-YOU

INTRODUCTION

Imagine you are listening to the news, or reading the local paper, and you come across something that fills you with rage or sadness, or just makes you want to scream. You want desperately to do something, to change things, to prevent further disaster, or to make things better.

Then the baby gets sick, you hit a crisis at work, the ESB bill comes, your relationship breaks down, it rains again, or you switch channels. You get distracted.

But whatever it is gnaws at your mind and just won't go away. So you think, 'It's terrible, why doesn't someone do something about it?'. You wait. Nothing happens

You tell yourself that you don't have the time to do anything anyway.

Then the story turns up again. Again, the hackles rise or the tears flow, only this time the seed of action is sown. You talk to a few people and they agree with you. You realise that you are all furious, sad or offended, and you wonder what to do about it.

So you arrange a meeting and people get excited. Plans are made, and, before you know it, you are strapped into a pilotless plane, screaming silently. The campaign has begun.

We know the feeling as we've been there quite a few times before, and it is that feeling which prompted us to write this book.

We hope that its contents will help to guide you through the process of setting up or developing your campaign, be it national, regional, or local, so that you reach your destination successfully. We hope that it will enthuse and empower those readers who may not yet be planning a campaign, and that it will provide some fresh insight and ideas for those who have been at it for years.

In a nutshell, our central message is that we, as ordinary people, can stand up and shout NO MORE! We have the power to create change. People can set up campaigns which will work if they are determined and organised enough to see them through. You just need good planning, a workable structure, some creative thinking and loads of energy. Add to this a pure belief in the justice of your cause and the determination to win. And of course, the ability to enjoy the ride!

To get the most from the book it should be read straight through. This will give you a good understanding of the need to integrate all aspects of your campaign. Alternatively, you might prefer to dip into chapters as the need arises. It can then be kept on the shelf for future reference.

After this, what else can we say but Good Luck!

1
PLANNING

'If one does not know to which port one is sailing, no wind is favourable.'

Seneca ('The Younger'), Roman philosopher and poet

'Tuas maith is leath na h-oibre' – A good start is half the work.

Irish proverb

INTRODUCTION

Usually a campaign will begin in a small room with a number of people coming together to influence or to prevent change. A bunch of excited and enthusiastic members is exactly what is needed, but before any progress can be made, you need to sit down and thrash out why you are all there, what you want to achieve, and how. The process of doing this will help everyone to get to know each other better, and to clarify for them what it is they are trying to do.

In this chapter we will be looking at the decisions which have to be made in this planning process.

ACTION PLAN
STRATEGY
AIMS
VISION

VISION

We often criticise policy-makers for not looking ahead and for making decisions without having a clear vision of the future in mind. Without vision, decisions tend to be made in a piecemeal fashion with little consideration of their long-term and spin-off effects.

So, when you are planning your campaign, it is important to work out in your mind a picture of how you would like things to be in the future. By doing this you will be putting your efforts into a much wider context. This picture will show what it is you are trying to work towards, as well as helping people to understand the wider implications of the issue.

AIMS

Once the overall vision is clear then you need to look more closely at what it is you are trying to achieve. What is the purpose of the campaign? This may be obvious if you are focusing on a single issue, but some campaigns may have a number of aims to work towards. Just be careful you don't list too many! The ones to concentrate on are those you can win. The rest could be added to a 'wish list' for the group to tackle at a later date.

Some groups may want to be tough and call these aims 'demands'; just be aware that strong language often turns people off, while wishy-washy words can get ignored.

Be careful not to confuse your aims. If you feel that a definite goal is attainable, focus clearly on it and don't include a secondary aim. If you give them a choice, the decision-makers are very likely to take the easiest option. On the other hand, if you feel your primary aim is definitely not possible to achieve now, then you may want to define this as a long-term aim, and include a target which is achievable in the short term as well. That way some sort of compromise can be reached.

CAMPAIGN STRATEGY

Once you have identified your aims, within the overall vision of the group, it's time to figure out how to achieve them. The strategy is the approach which the group will take, and sets the framework for all campaigning effort. In setting direction for your group, it is important to firstly identify your campaign type and the campaign targets.

Type of Campaign

The type of campaign you run is jointly dictated by your aims and your chosen strategy. Some elements of campaign type, such as public acceptability, will be fixed at the beginning, while others, like the number of issues to work on, can be set by the group as part of your strategy.

Proactive or Reactive? – A proactive campaign is one in which you are initiating change. The situation will remain the same unless you do something about it. This usually means that you can proceed from one stage to another at your own pace.

A reactive campaign involves responding to change. This might be a planning proposal, discontinuation of a local service or some form of legislative change.

Publicly Acceptable or Unacceptable? – A publicly acceptable campaign has a message which attracts plenty of support, making it easier to lobby politicians and gather funds.

An unacceptable campaign is one which attracts widespread opposition. You must therefore put a lot more effort into tailoring your message and your aims, so that you get as much support as possible. People may be less keen to get involved, and raising funds could be more difficult. The key to success in this case is to be patient and to work gradually, always putting forward your arguments with sincerity and conviction, taking into consideration the fears of your opponents.

Single Issue or a Number of Different Issues? – A single-issue campaign is, by its nature, very focused. All your resources and energies are targeted towards the one goal.

If your campaign is dealing with a number of issues, you may have to put more thought into the structure and overall co-ordination of the campaign, so that the different issues get dealt with adequately.

Short-term or Ongoing? – A short-term campaign is set up in the knowledge that the aims are achievable in a short period of time, and that when this occurs the campaign group will disband.

An on-going campaign is one which is expected to continue for a substantial length of time, and which will have a more permanent existence. This has a bearing on practical decisions, such as employing people and office space.

Campaign Targets

Once you know what your group wants, you must work out who can give it to you. Who are to be the 'targets' of the campaign and how best can you get to them?

'The Powers That Be' – Target with Power. Who holds the power to change the situation? What is the chain of command above them? Who might hold power in the near future, or further on in the process?

You will want to work out ways of influencing those in power.

'Rogues' – Target for Blame. Who is responsible for the problems? It might be the people who created a situation, or those who maintain it.

It might be possible to convert them to your way of thinking, or you may want to publicly shame and discredit them.

'The Troops' – Target for Public Support. What sections of the community will support the campaign? Factors to consider include geographical area, age group, lifestyle and income. People directly affected might provide the best base.

By identifying the target group, you can expect maximum return for your efforts in seeking support.

'Allies' – Target For Assistance. What other campaign or community groups agree with your campaign message? What groups or businesses stand to benefit from the success of your campaign?

A diversity of groups signed on to your cause will broaden interest and support, as well as bringing more pressure to bear.

'Rivals' – Target for Resistance. It is important to clarify this early on as it should give you an idea of where opposition could come from.

Identifying such targets well in advance allows you to work out ways of winning them over by reassurance or compromise, or to undermine their position by strong campaigning. You might even discover suspect business or political interests which could be exposed at some appropriate time.

Devising Your Strategy

Having figured out all of the major components of the campaign, and all of the likely players, it is time to develop a strategy. This consists of your overall 'plan of attack' – the general approach which will be taken to achieve your aims. Your strategy is the skeleton around which you build your campaign, fleshing it out with tactics.

Looking at a few examples will show how simple or complex your strategy can be:-

- A group dealing with the issue of contaminated blood products might decide to just focus on the Department of Health, identifying them as the 'Rogues' and the 'Powers that Be'.

- A group trying to save a building in their area, which the public wants cleared away for a new factory, might split their approach. While working on the issue of saving the building, they might separately campaign for improvements to the whole area. The hope would be that the bad publicity of the first issue could be offset by being seen to be proactive in trying to bring about favourable change in the area. The strategy would be to win over the 'Rivals', and maybe even turn them into 'Allies' or 'Troops'.

- A group trying to prevent a dirty industry from setting up in their area might identify them as the 'Rogue' and encourage them to establish a plant there only if it could be made to operate cleanly. Failing this, the group might move on to gathering support through a wide range of 'Allies' and strong 'Troops', and bringing pressure to bear on whatever 'Powers that Be' had the power to stop it.

As part of your strategy, you will want to decide how to present your group and message to the public. The image which you create will affect how well your strategy works. (See Chapter 6: Promotion of the Group and Message.)

ACTION PLAN

By the time you have all of that figured out, you should be champing at the bit to get your action plan together. This is where you plan out all the activities and events which you intend to use to achieve your aims. It sets the agenda for your work, and allows you to see what resources you require well in advance. It is the basis for developing further plans in the areas of fund-raising, the media and lobbying.

Developing the Action Plan

Within the framework set by your Aims and Strategy, the group can get together and brainstorm ideas for, say, a three month period. From this, you decide what can realistically be organised during that time-frame, and what would be most beneficial to the campaign.

Action Plans are the fun part of Planning, as you figure what activities, meetings and protest events you will organise and set deadlines for the production of leaflets and promotional material.

It may be a good idea to get out the thick markers, draw monthly calendars on large sheets of paper, one month per sheet, and stick them on the wall. Once activities are agreed upon, mark them into the appropriate time-slot.

While it is really important to plan ahead, no calendar of events can be rigid. Sometimes campaigns take on a life of their own, and you will find that the best laid plans often get thrown out the window, to be replaced by a frenzy of unexpected activity and potential chaos. The secret is to set plans based on realistic timing and where possible to expect the unexpected. Keep your ears to the ground so that you are aware of what the opposition is planning. Be flexible and always have room for emergency action.

Resources Available

Be realistic when you are working out your plan. Take into account the resources available to your group, in terms of people-power, expertise, money, premises, practical equipment, access to free favours and cheaper services.

Don't be put off if at first it looks like these are pretty thin on the ground. The golden rule is to work out what you really need to win the campaign, and if the necessary resources are not readily available, then you go out of your way to find them. Obviously, as the campaign develops, becomes more credible and support increases, what you need will be much easier to come by.

Budget

Alongside the Action Plan, you need to work out a Budget to cover the costs of your activities, administration and office equipment. Obviously some of this will include a bit of guesswork, but it will give you an idea of how much money you will need in order to function. It will also encourage you to think realistically about money from the start and to develop a fund-raising plan alongside the Action Plan.

Keep the budget simple. If you feel you really haven't a clue how much various items will cost, it's a good idea to get advice from someone who has experience of campaigning or of running similar groups.

SAMPLE BUDGET

Budget for the period Jan 1 – March 31 1999

Projected income	£	*Projected expenditure*	£
Cake Sale	200	Leaflet printing	300
Street collection (hopefully!)	1,100	Purchase of T-shirts (100 @ £4)	400
Sale of T-shirts (100 @ £6)	600	Public march	150
Donations	300	Stationery and stamps	50
Appeal on leaflets	800	Telephone	150
		Travel	100
		Legal Fees	850
		Other expenses	100
		Carry over next period	900
	3,000		3,000

Cost of Leaflet printing will need to be paid early in period, so the Cake Sale must take place beforehand, and some of the promised donations will need to be followed up. The Appeal will be in the middle of February, and the Street collection at the beginning of March, which will cover the other expenses as they arise.

It is important that your Treasurer keeps on top of the Budget, updates it when necessary and ensures a good cash flow so that the group does not blindly land itself in debt. Figures from the actual income and expenditure of the group should be compared with the Budget for that period, in order to give you an idea of whether your estimates were accurate or wildly off the mark. This will help to ensure that your future predictions are more precise.

EVALUATION

Regular evaluation provides the feedback by which you can judge
the success of your activities.

It lets the group look at how or whether it is achieving its aims,
and recognize any factors which have held up progress, enabling
you to make any necessary changes. In practical terms this may
mean looking at which activities have gone well and which have
failed, working out the reasons why, and including what you have
learnt in future plans.

As a result of such evaluation you may decide that the direction
of the campaign is going a little off-course and moving further
away from the overall aims. Maybe you need to change the priority
of your objectives, to revise your strategy, to re-structure the group,
to focus on different targets, to raise and spend more money, or, if
your work is done, to just close down.

Regular evaluation sessions will also help to forewarn you of
some potential crises. This gives you time to prevent them
occurring, or if they are unavoidable, to at least put in place the
mechanisms for dealing with them effectively.

This process of looking back over what combination of factors
affected your success should be applied throughout your work,
right up to the end. Once your campaign has been won (hopefully!),
remember to sit down and see how you can apply what you have
learned to new situations, or share it with other groups.

ANECDOTE: UCD BABY MILK ACTION

Baby Milk Action *is an organisation campaigning for a complete boycott of Nestle's products in response to the company's marketing practices in the developing world..*

Before **Baby Milk Action** (re)launched the Nestlé Boycott in Ireland, the One World Society in UCD was already actively raising awareness in the college. After a successful information week in September 1994, it was suggested that the Students Union remove Nestle products from the SU shop. This couldn't be done without a mandate from the students and a referendum was proposed. This hadn't been part of the original plan, but it was decided that a referendum would be the best way to make a statement to Nestle and a campaign was born.

Postponed until the following term, the date was set for the 10th of November and the planning began. Under Student Union rules, campaigning cannot begin until the week before the vote. All the planning had to be done for this one hectic week. Some groundwork was done organising information meetings (with speakers from Baby Milk Action) about the issue before the campaign began. The campaign had two objectives – to remove Nestle products from the shops and to raise as much awareness as possible.

Sparse funding had been allocated in the most effective way. It was decided that the most important part of the campaign was information and a lot of effort went into ensuring that everything claimed was accurate, consistent and conveyed in a rational, rather than emotive, way. The manifesto was a well-planned document which laid the facts down concisely and convincingly, using respected sources such as WHO and UNICEF and stressing positive action. Flyers and posters were designed using the same attractive image as the manifesto for easy recognition. There was an information stand throughout the week.

Taking all the advice available from experienced student camapigners, lecture addresses were planned and divided up between members of the campaign team. Working in four teams of two, all the faculties and most of the residences were covered. Chatting to people was very effective and most of the feedback was good, although some were more ready to listen than others – a student making a lecture address to a business class was pelted with oranges!

Despite an anti-boycott campaign, the hard work of the boycott team and the strength of the message paid off. The boycott was carried and UCD Students Union shops no longer stock Nestle products – so planning and people power do make a difference, no matter what your budget.

2
STRUCTURE

'Give me but one firm spot on which to stand, and I will move the earth.'

Archimedes, Greek mathematician and inventor

'Looking at the Earth from afar you realize it is too small for conflict and just big enough for co-operation.'

Yuri Gagarin, Cosmonaut

INTRODUCTION

Creating a workable structure within which to run a lively campaign is a bit like setting good foundations before building a house – the whole thing will collapse if the right base isn't there.

Just as foundations are crucial to the entire building, the structure you set up has to serve the campaign and its members as a whole, not specific individuals. On the other hand, you don't want the structure to become more important than the campaign itself, so you need to find a happy balance.

This chapter aims to give you an understanding of how best to put a group together. It will take you through decision-making, financial and legal structures, as well as the mundane, but important, issues of office space and equipment.

HOW DECISIONS ARE MADE

The founding members of the campaign group will probably begin to meet on a regular basis, with everyone doing a bit of everything, and the odd new member joining along the way. Things could be going so well that you feel there is no need to set up a Committee or to take on any formal structure. If the group remains small, the campaign is very focused, pressure from outside is limited and no 'egos' emerge, then a loose structure like this may indeed work. On the other hand, as things develop and more people get involved, this structure can be the cause of some major interpersonal and organisational problems which will take a lot of energy and time to sort out.

To prevent this from happening, and to give the group more credibility, it is a wise move to *set structures in place at an early stage*, beginning with the Co-ordinating Committee.

The formality of a Committee with named positions may seem a bit much at first, but as well as showing that you are well organised, it is especially important if you are setting up a Limited Company, or looking for central funding from statutory or other sources.

The Co-ordinating Committee

When the initial group meets to discuss planning and the way forward, it's best to set up a Temporary Committee with people filling the roles of Chairperson, Secretary and Treasurer. This group gets the campaign up and running, takes it through the early planning stages, and sets the appropriate structures for wider participation.

Once more people have become involved, you know each other better, and the direction of the campaign is clearer, you should hold a meeting to put together a more permanent formation. At this meeting the structure is worked out, and it is agreed (and maybe voted on) who will become Committee Officers. If people are not willing to take on a position of responsibility, you could decide what sort of person or skills you need and then after a bit of local scouting, encourage them to join the group.

Functions

The Co-ordinating Committee represents all the group members, including volunteers and any paid workers, and is responsible for the overall running and direction of the campaign.

An effective Committee is constantly making sure there is a good flow of information between itself and the group's members. This includes getting feedback from them in order to represent their views in making decisions.

Further functions of the Co-ordinating Committee include:-

- Taking responsibility for any legal matters.
- Being accountable for all the money going in and out.
- Making overall policy decisions or changes.
- Taking on the role of employer for any paid workers.

Size

The size of the Committee will depend a lot on the type of campaign you are running. However, it's best not to let it get too big – anything over twelve is likely to be difficult to manage and will require a large room for meetings. On the other hand, anything under six may not be enough to cover all the jobs.

Co-ordinating Committee Members

If possible, your Committee should include a good mix of personalities and skills, with everyone pulling their weight. Try to avoid the 'talkers' who disappear as soon as any work needs to be done.

While it is up to you to decide what positions are necessary and what each person is to do, the following officer roles are the most common:-

Chairperson – A good Chair is crucial to the running of a successful campaign. As well as planning and running Committee meetings, the Chair provides the overall leadership for the group. This involves a lot of tact and sensitivity, as well as the ability to take a strong stance if needed. An ideal Chair is a person who leads from behind, encouraging people to take part and to accept responsibilities (both in meetings and in the wider group). They should make sure that the group sticks to its policies and gets everything done, while also trying to avoid any tensions or interpersonal conflicts.

Secretary – The Secretary is generally responsible for taking minutes at meetings, for sending out (or at least signing) important letters, for circulating agendas and other Committee material, and for making sure all in-coming post is dealt with and filed. The role suits a person who is conscientious, reliable and who is particular about getting things just right. Attention to detail is important especially when minutes and correspondence are concerned.

Treasurer – The Treasurer manages the finances of the group but doesn't necessarily have to be involved in actually raising them. They ensure that proper financial records are kept and they usually sign cheques. Although a person does not have to be a mathematical genius to take on this job, it helps if they are interested in figures and meticulous in keeping the books straight and paying bills promptly.

Press Officer – The Press Officer co-ordinates all the media events for the campaign and is the person who contacts the press and arranges interviews. They may not necessarily be a campaign spokesperson, but this helps as often reporters want a quick comment. For this role you need someone with a good manner who can get across the importance of the cause and the need for coverage, without being too pushy. The person should also have a thick neck and plenty of patience, as often they will be dealing with hassled journalists or editors rushing for a deadline. They should be organised, to make sure that all press materials are sent out on time.

Campaign Co-ordinator – The Co-ordinator is the person who pulls together the various strands of your campaign, making sure that everything happens according to plan in between Committee meetings. (For further information on this position, see Chapter 3: Campaigners.)

Sub-Groups

Depending on the size of your campaign and how it develops, you may find that it is a good idea to split into a number of working sub-groups, which will each focus on their own area of activity. That way the time, specific skills and interests of campaign volunteers can be put to their best use. Such areas could include Media Relations, Fund-Raising, Promotion and Legal Issues. As new volunteers appear they can join the sub-group(s) of their choice (you will probably find that some people end up wearing a few different hats).

Each sub-group has its own work sessions and a representative attends the Co-ordinating Committee meetings. While taking part in overall decision-making and voicing the views of their group, the sub-group representative also plays the part of a channel, informing the overall Committee of their activities, and ensuring that they are approved. They then feed back to the sub-group the activities of other work groups and the decisions made at the Committee meeting. This way people should feel they have a say in the running of the campaign. Every so often it is a good idea to have an open meeting where everyone gets together to thrash out certain issues and to make decisions relating to the development of the campaign.

Co-opted members of the Co-ordinating Committee

While you shouldn't underestimate your own abilities or knowledge and your power to change things without outside help, you may want to bring someone with special areas of expertise or specific skills onto the Committee now and then. This might be a person who could give sound legal advice, a PR expert, someone with business or direct action experience or someone with political knowledge. If you are inviting anyone to join the Committee be sure that this is fully agreed by the others, and that you all feel content about the person in question. However, try not to let the Committee become too big.

Executive Committee

It's always best to avoid situations where people have to make important decisions on their own. Making an individual decision can put a lot of pressure on one person, who is then likely to be blamed if things go wrong. It also leaves the door open for that person's opinions to outweigh those of others, which may lead to a lot of discontent and problems.

Therefore, it's a good idea to agree on an Executive Committee, maybe two or three people who are available and whom the Co-ordinating Committee have chosen to make quick decisions outside of meetings. You might be surprised how often this need arises. A quick ring around and discussion amongst three people is much easier than trying to involve all Committee members in the decision at short notice. The existence of an Executive Committee is very helpful and supportive to the Campaign Co-ordinator or Chairperson, on whose door-step the urgent situation most often gets landed.

CAMPAIGN BASE

Options

Early on, give some thought to where your campaign base will be. Decisions will depend on the size of the campaign, its needs, and its expected development. Do you require a base for the Campaign Co-ordinator or voluntary office staff, a space for meetings, or just a phone line?

The following are a number of options:

A contact telephone number and address

This is *the bare minimum required* for any campaign, in order to be accessible to the outside world. If resources allow, rather than using someone's personal line, it is a good idea to install a special phone line into a member's house or office and to attach an answering machine or service so that messages can be left if no-one is around. Having an answering machine also means you don't have to be continually 'on duty'. You can answer messages in your own time or you can sit by the phone and screen the calls! The latter may be necessary if your campaign is attracting a number of nuisance calls.

You need to think carefully when deciding upon a contact address. Usually this goes out on the group's headed paper and informational material, and so becomes widely available. Someone on your Committee may be willing to use their own home address, or you could have your post sent to the local Community Centre or another friendly organisation. It is also possible to organise a Post Box Number, so that all mail goes to your local sorting office, and awaits collection, but be aware that this can appear very anonymous, and sometimes gives the impression that the group members don't want to be located.

Meeting Space

You may need to find space for Committee or work group meetings. It could be more convenient if all these meetings don't have to be in the same place. You may find that it works to hold Committee meetings in members' houses, on a rota basis. A local pub may offer an upstairs room for work-group or open meetings, with a view to people socialising afterwards in the bar, or you may get the use of a room from a friendly organisation or Community Centre.

Rent-Free Office Space

If you need to have some sort of administrative base, or at least somewhere with a desk, a phone and a filing cabinet, it's well worth asking around to see if anything is available rent-free. Try your local Community Centre, Church, Arts Centre or other groups in the area. A member of your group may have a spare room, or a corner at work which could be used. If you are employing a Campaign Co-ordinator, they might be willing to work from their own home.

Rented Office

If you are unable to find a free office, and your finances are healthy enough, you could look for a rented space. But, be careful! Try to pick its location to suit your campaign's needs. Upstairs is cheaper, but it's no good if you want to be accessible to the public and need a ground floor window for displaying merchandise and group information. On the other hand, you may be better off upstairs if you don't have enough volunteers to facilitate a drop-in service. Do you want to be in the city or town centre, or more locally based?

Administrative Equipment

Computer

It is essential to have something to type on – a word processor, or better still a good computer and printer. Many people, particularly politicians and the media, make quick judgments about a group based on the material they have to hand. If your letter or Press Release is well laid out and typed, then it is much more likely to be read than a scrawled note on crumpled paper. Apart from looking well, it is also a lot easier to read, a blessing for harried journalists or political secretaries.

If you manage to lay hands on a computer, try not to get one that uses an unusual package which is incompatible with other machines, in case you need to transfer material at some stage. Once you have a computer, it's worth investing in a modem. This is a device which enables your computer to send and receive information over the phone line, allowing you to link in to E-Mail and the Internet. (See Chapter 4: Accessing Information.)

Fax Machine

A fax machine is very useful, as it facilitates quick contact with people, and is invaluable when you are organising Press events or trying to get information quickly to the press and politicians.

If you cannot afford one, borrowing or leasing are options. Better still, if you have a computer and modem, you will be able to send faxes directly to another computer.

Photocopier

As they are very expensive, it is unlikely that your group will be interested in buying one – although leasing is always an option if you feel it would be worth it. Alternatively, you can look around and see who provides a cheap photocopying service or do a deal with another group. Some of your group members may have access to free photocopying which is great for bulk amounts, but for

day-to-day use it is more practical to have a source close to your
campaign base.

Office Procedures

If you have an office base, and a number of workers or volunteers
using it, good office procedures and methods of recording are
particularly important. This helps to keep tabs on paperwork, and
on who is doing what.

Use of the Phone

If more than one person is using the phone and you are worried
about ending up with a hefty phone bill, it is a good idea to have a
Phone Book for recording all calls and their estimated length. If
people have to do this, they are less likely to stay on the line for too
long. Put a Phone Box nearby to accept the money for personal calls.
An itemised bill will also help you to keep track of phone expenses.
    It is possible to set your phone for local or national calls only.

Letters in/out

As letters come in they should be logged in a Letters-In Book,
clearly noting the date of receipt, and what response, if any, is
required. At the back of the book you can record the dates of all
outgoing mail, and the name of the sender. This procedure is very
useful if you ever want to check whether something has been sent
off, or received, and by whom. Keep copies of all outgoing letters
in your files for future reference.
    If mail comes in for a number of different people, it's worth getting
a set of trays and labelling them with their names, or constructing
some sort of 'pigeon hole' system, so that letters can easily be
directed to the right people.

Filing System

A filing cabinet is extremely useful for storing information. They're
quite expensive to buy new, but a hunt around second hand shops
can reduce the cost. Better still, you may be able to scrounge an old
one from someone's office. A lick of paint and you're away! How
you name and order your files really depends on who is setting up
the system. Just be sure that everyone knows how it works. If you
are holding any confidential material, you should store it in a locked
drawer, and only give keys to the people who really need them.

Diary

It is a good idea to mark all forthcoming meetings, press events, training sessions and other campaign activities in a Diary. As well as serving as a reminder, it can inform people at a glance of what is going on in the campaign. It is also useful to be able to look back in a Diary to confirm a date or to check up on when a particular event occurred.

Message Book

So that messages, phone messages in particular, don't get lost, you should have a special recording book, listing who called, for whom, and any message or return phone number.

Contact Lists

A central address book is handy, so that all useful addresses and phone numbers are easily accessible to whoever needs them. Little pieces of paper just don't work, no matter how much we try to convince ourselves!

It's also a good idea to put together a list of the Committee members (with mailing addresses and home/work phone numbers) and also lists of volunteers, supporters, supporting organisations, patrons and whoever else might be relevant. These need to be regularly updated as people join or leave.

FINANCIAL SYSTEM

Operating a strict financial recording system is really important, so that everyone inside the campaign is aware of what is going on financially. It is also necessary so that people on the outside, the donors, funding organisations and the general public, can rest assured that their money is being well managed and accounted for. Sometimes, allegations or rumours relating to dubious sources of funding, or the internal filching of money, emerge, particularly when the campaign pressure is hurting someone! A well-kept set of books and audited accounts, open for scrutiny, should serve to dispel such accusations.

Bank Account

The first move is to set up a campaign bank account. If you have any contacts in a particular bank, it's a good idea to join that bank, in case you need any advice or run into problems. Alternatively, build up a relationship with the Manager as soon as you can. For convenience, try to pick a branch near your campaign base. Open a current account, but if you find you raise surplus money at any stage you could also open a deposit account.

You will have to fill out a number of forms, and give sample signatures of the people who are authorised to sign cheques. As no cheque cards are given with group accounts, two signatures are required on each cheque. Most groups name three or four people, including the Treasurer, Chairperson and/or Co-ordinator, with any two signing at one time.

Petty Cash

If you want money for small day-to-day expenses, get a Petty Cash Box and work out who will have access to the key. At regular intervals, or whenever you need to, use a cheque to move money into it from your account. Make sure that all expenditures are logged into a Petty Cash Book, and all are matched by a corresponding receipt.

It's a good idea to stick or staple the receipts onto A4 sheets of paper, and to keep them in a ring-binder in date order.

Alternatively, if people are willing to buy the items out of their own money, they may file the receipts and then receive a cheque to cover their costs on a regular basis.

Book-keeping

Rather than going into detail here on how to set up and run a good book-keeping system, it's best if your Treasurer takes advice from an accountant or an experienced book-keeper. Depending on your resources they may want to work on computer spreadsheets, or just use a manual book system to record all monies coming in and going out.

Auditing

If you're running a long-term campaign, and particularly if you are a Limited Company, you will need to have your books checked by a qualified auditor once a year. This means that your Treasurer's formal statement of Accounts will be verified by an outsider, and you will receive a statement confirming that they are an accurate representation of your group's finances.

Other Points

- Always get receipts for any money spent, even for the smallest petty cash payment. For future reference, mark the date and what was bought on the receipt if this is not clear.

- Give receipts for all money received.

- Avoid large cash payments, use cheques wherever possible.

- All donations should be lodged, using a lodgment book. Never spend a donation without putting it into your account first, so that everything goes through the books.

- Be sure to fill out all lodgment and cheque stubs.

- Don't sign blank cheques!

LEGAL ISSUES

Once there is a good idea of what the group is about and how it aims to work, some thought needs to be given to setting up some form of legal framework. Time spent on this at the beginning should avoid many of the problems which can arise as the campaign develops.

Group Solicitor

At an early stage you should try to link up with a friendly solicitor, who will act as your legal advisor throughout the campaign. Hopefully you will be able to find someone with a personal interest in the cause who will take on this role free of charge, or at least work at a very reduced rate. If not, you need to be very clear about potential costs, so that you don't end up with a huge bill for what you thought were just a few friendly chats!

Your solicitor should be well equipped to advise on whether or not to put a legal structure in place, and on which to choose. This will very much depend on the type and extent of your campaign, its expected time-span, your financial situation, any plans to take legal action, whether you employ people and the views of your members.

Legal Structure

This is a recognised formal structure, within which the group will operate, such as a group governed by a constitution.

Having a legal structure offers a number of advantages to a group:-

- It ensures that you formalise the aims, rules and decision-making structure of the group, rather than leaving these issues to verbal agreements which can be quickly forgotten or overturned.

- It helps to maintain stability where there is a high turnover of members.

- It is a requirement for some potential funding bodies.

- It can give the group more credibility with banks and other institutions.

- It can show people that you are really serious about your campaign, and that you are planning to be around for a while.

Legal Status

Legal status gives the group a distinct legal existence and is a step up from having only a legal structure.

Incorporating as a company limited by guarantee is the main way for a campaign group to get legal status. A group might find that legal structure alone is not enough, that it requires some of the further benefits that legal status offers.

Advantages of legal status:-

- It gives members some degree of protection from liability for debts incurred by the campaign.

- The group can employ people and hold property in its own right.

- The group can take part in the legal system in its own right.

- Some potential funding bodies require a group to have legal status.

Charitable Status

This is a separate issue from legal structure or legal status. A group with charitable status is recognised as charitable by the Revenue Commissioners for tax purposes. The benefits come in the form of exemption from certain taxes and an improved chance of finance from funding organisations. Legal status is not essential to acquire charitable status. Application must be made to the Revenue Commissioners who will give details of the criteria for groups and the information they require to make a decision. If you think your group could benefit from this then it is worthwhile sending off for details.

SUGGESTED STRUCTURES

Group governed by a constitution

One of the easiest ways for a group to operate is by drawing up a constitution, which lays out the rules under which it will be run. It needs to be thought out and carefully worded, with the help of your solicitor, to suit your own particular needs. A Constitution creates an agreement between members of your group, and helps to prevent internal squabbles.

This gives the group a legal structure, but not legal status. Therefore individual members of the group cannot be protected from the possibility of legal action if the campaign runs into debt. Don't be put off by this – many groups happily exist on this level, and if your finances are well managed then the prospect of ending up as debtors should be very remote indeed.

It's a good idea to have a look at a few Constitutions drawn up by other groups to get an idea of possible content. Broadly, most will probably contain the following:-

- Group's aims
- How to achieve these
- Organisation of membership
- Decision-making structure
- Committee powers
- How officers are elected
- Voting rights
- Frequency of meetings
- Date of Annual General Meeting
- Management of finances
- How to wind up the campaign
- Procedures for altering the Constitution.

Company Limited by Guarantee

By incorporating as a company, without share capital, a group gets both a legal structure and legal status. This involves a bit more work and money, although having a friendly solicitor should keep the costs down.

The aims of the group must be drawn up in the document called the Memorandum of Association. Its rules on decision-making structures, financial management, membership and so on must go in the Articles of Association. A further form (form A1, available from the Companies Registration Office) should give details of directors and the address of the registered office. These three documents must be submitted to the Companies Office in Dublin, along with the fee (currently at I£145).

Further responsibilities that go with incorporation include sending audited accounts to the Companies Office each year, along with details of any changes to the information already supplied.

HOW TO RUN EFFECTIVE COMMITTEE OR OTHER GROUP MEETINGS

A well-run Committee meeting can be both enjoyable and productive, and, if it ends promptly, you will still have time afterwards to head to the pub for a drink. However, not all meetings run smoothly. The following are common problems which can emerge:-

- Meetings drag on for ages and everyone starts to get fed-up, worn out and cranky.

- People talk too long and ramble off on tangents.

- The discussion seems to go round in circles without any proper decisions being made.

- Decisions are made but no-one is too sure who is to carry them out.

- Disagreements arise which can then turn into blazing rows.

In order to run more effective meetings, thought needs to be given to the following points:-

Frequency

Firstly, you need to decide how often you should meet – this will probably depend on what stage of the campaign you are at. You may need to have weekly meetings if a lot is happening, or if you're going through a quiet patch, once a month might be enough.

Timing

Set a start time, and try to be punctual, even if only a few people turn up. Once a precedent is set, soon enough all the members will know that if they're not there on time they will miss something.

Set an end time. A two-hour meeting is long enough, particularly after a tiring day. Anything over that means that issues get poorly discussed and decisions are made in a hurry because people are worn out and just dying to get out that door. If it looks like more discussion is needed and the decision can wait, put the item on the top of the agenda for the next meeting, or if it is more urgent, schedule another meeting.

Ground Rules

At the first meeting set the ground rules which people feel are appropriate. These could relate to whether or not people can smoke at meetings, punctuality, the importance of listening and not interrupting, completion of tasks and following through on responsibilities.

Preparation

Before each meeting a certain amount of planning needs to be done. This ensures that there is some order to the meeting and all necessary issues are covered. An agenda is a key document.

The Chairperson, with the Co-ordinator or Secretary's help, should prepare and circulate the agenda in advance of the meeting. This means that, on arrival, Committee members will know what is to be discussed. Be sure to leave a space for Any Other Business, so that important issues which have been forgotten can be included.

When setting out the Agenda, it is important to bear in mind the length of the meeting and to try to include only those issues which really need to be discussed. To get the most from any meeting, *good time management is essential.* Put the simple items at the top so that they are dealt with quickly and leave time for the more complicated issues. However, you need to be flexible with this – if some Committee members cannot stay until the end of the meeting, it's best to take the more important matters first.

Meeting Space

It is important to try to meet in a room which suits the size of your Committee, and to make sure that there are enough chairs for everyone. Most groups find it more comfortable to sit in a semi-circle, or to all sit around a table, rather than having the Officers behind a desk facing the others.

Direction

The role of the Chairperson comes into its own here. Without dominating, they guide and control the meeting while making sure that each person has a chance to speak and to be heard. It requires great tact and a firm hand to make sure that the meeting keeps moving, that it isn't side-tracked from the agenda, and that people don't waste valuable time. When contentious issues have to be discussed, the Chairperson needs to make sure that a decision or compromise is reached without some people feeling their views have not been taken into consideration.

After each item the Chair should clarify what has been agreed and who is to take responsibility for carrying out the decision. This clarification is particularly helpful for the person taking the minutes.

Before the meeting begins, it is useful to set aside a short while for an informal chat and to 'check in' with people. This will give everyone a chance to say something before the meeting begins, which should encourage greater participation later on. It can also give people an idea of what sort of moods the other Committee members are in, enabling better understanding of why people may be a bit cranky during the meeting itself.

Minutes

Usually the Secretary takes the minutes. As well as being a useful record for future reference, they *must be kept if you are a Limited Company*. Minutes need not be word-for-word transcripts of the whole meeting. It is enough to clearly record who attended, the main items discussed and the decisions reached. It is a good idea to send them out to members, so that they will have already been read and only need to be ratified at the next meeting, saving valuable discussion time.

ANECDOTE: SAFE COMMUNICATIONS COUNCIL
PLUGGING THE DIKE, A NATIONAL STORY

The **Safe Communications Council** *grew out of a local campaign against a single mast in West Waterford and moved on to tackle the issue on a national scale.*

Remember the story of the little Dutch boy who plugged the dike with his finger? He saw the danger, rose to the occasion, the community supported him, and everyone lived happily ever after.

Except, that after averting that first environmental disaster, the little Dutch boy found that he kept having to plug more and ever more leaky holes. It got tiresome.

When our little band of Irish boys and girls successfully fought off a mast on top of our local Comeragh Mountains, we found ourselves immediately facing an inundation of similar, often ill-conceived proposals. What started as a single issue turned into a constant battle against a flood of developer's proposals. We were drowning.

So we took the fight nationwide.

Dealing with our little patch was not stemming the tide. One thousand and two hundred mobile phone masts are being erected around the country as well as hundreds of microwave TV and radio masts. We became aware that all round Ireland dozens of little local groups were fighting the exact same sort of battle. We figured if we stood united, we'd have a better chance of winning some sort of safe, rational, national communications plan.

A meeting was called. We telephoned everyone we know that was fighting this issue. We were looking for just a few key people from each of the local groups, not a mass public meeting. We set a date, picked a reasonably central location (County Tipperary), drew up an agenda, and set off to see who would turn up.

At our first meeting, 55 dike pluggers turned up, representing 20 groups from 16 counties. We swapped horror stories, elected an executive committee, and combined ideas to form a complete programme we could propose to the government.

Thanks to the miracle of computers and faxes, we could send out our first press release nationwide. Every radio station and newspaper in the country received our first press release. Within days the chairman of our new national group was giving interviews on radio. RTÉ TV has done two specials featuring members of our group. Dozens of articles appeared in the press.

Our second press release followed a month later. Again, it caused a stir. Marian Finucane took an interest and three broadcasts were devoted to the issue. The Minister of the Environment was questioned in the last of these. We've met with TDs. Meetings with key officials in the Department of the Environment and Communications were arranged.

Since we're still in the middle of things, we don't know how it will turn out. But, we are being heard! Ireland is, thankfully, a democracy, and if our representatives want to keep their jobs, they have to keep their ears open.

So – advice? If it's a national issue, then take it national. It gives heart to all the local fighters to know they're not alone, and gives substance to your dealings with government and press. Just maybe, when all is finished, the little Irish lads and cailíní will indeed be able to live happily ever after.

Scott Simons, Secretary, Safe Communications Council.

Since the above article was written, Department of the Environment policy and the Telecommunications Bill have been influenced by the campaigning and recommendations of the group.

3
THE CAMPAIGNERS

*'The humblest citizen of all the land, when clad in the armor of a
righteous cause, is stronger than all the hosts of war.'*
William Jennings Bryan, American politician.

INTRODUCTION

Any campaign will only be as good as the people taking part.

When a group is working well together, all efforts can be focused
on achieving the campaign aims.

If this happens naturally – great! More often, it needs some
thought and understanding from those involved in the running of
the campaign.

This chapter aims to give you that understanding, looking at the
needs of the group, and of those who choose to get involved. The
first part of the chapter will look at the practicalities of getting
people into the team and working with them. The second part
examines the way people relate to each other in campaign group
situations, and how to keep everything as smooth as possible.

VOLUNTEERS

Unless your campaign is very small and focused, you will probably
want to bring more volunteers into the fold. In this section, we look
at the needs of these new volunteers, and at ways in which your
organising committee can best recruit, train and support them.

Why People May Want to Volunteer

People will join your group for a variety of reasons. They may feel
very strongly about the issue you are campaigning on, or they may
be personally affected by it. Some may want to do something useful
in their spare time, or to gain new skills and experience, while
others may hope to meet like-minded people and to make new
friends. Most will want to enjoy themselves along the way.

It's a good idea to ask people at the outset why they are offering their help, and what they expect from the group. That way you will hopefully be able to understand and respond to their individual needs.

What Volunteers Need

While people will often have specific expectations of their involvement in the group, there are certain needs which are general to everyone. If these are catered for, the campaign is bound to run more smoothly.

All volunteers need to be given a clear idea of what is expected of them, and what tasks they are to fulfill.

- They need to feel secure that the group is being well-managed and that their involvement is not likely to be abused.

- They need to feel that their skills are recognised and used.

- They should have a say in the running of the campaign and be included in the decision-making process.

- They need to know to whom they are accountable, and to whom they can go for help or support.

- They should be given respect, appreciation and a thank-you now and then.

- All their expenses connected with the campaign should be willingly covered.

- They should receive a sense of fulfilment and accomplishment from their involvement, and not be given all the boring jobs.

Volunteer Co-ordinator

One of the best ways of looking after your volunteers, and hopefully encouraging as many as possible to stick with the campaign, is to have a Volunteer Co-ordinator, whose role is to make sure that their needs are properly met by the group.

Recruitment

Role of the Volunteers

Before you look for volunteers, you need to have a good idea of what you want them to do and what role they will have in the group's decision-making. This should be easy enough if you have clearly worked out your aims, strategy and structure. Prepare a list of practical tasks for people to do, as well as particular skills you may be looking for. Try to be flexible so that you can use all the talents people offer.

How many

Usually groups are keen to get as many people involved as possible, but if you feel you are not prepared for an influx of volunteers it is best to decide on a cut-off figure. Be sure to allow for the natural process of self-selection, where people opt out themselves over time.

How to get them

Word of mouth usually brings in quite a few people, particularly if existing members rope in their friends and acquaintances. It's a good idea to include a support coupon on all your leaflets, newsletters and informational material, asking people if they wish to volunteer. (See Chapter 6: Promotion of the Group and Message.)

You can also send appeals through the local newspapers, or radio station, and put up posters in shops and on public notice boards. Friendly organisations could be asked to pass the word around, and don't forget to encourage people to sign up after any public meeting or talk.

People who are unemployed can fill in a form, available from the labour exchange, which allows them to do voluntary work and continue to sign on.

Selection

Your Volunteer Co-ordinator may want to have an informal chat or interview with interested volunteers before they become involved in the group. This could be particularly important if the campaign is of a sensitive or confidential nature. If you decide to do this, you need to be clear on what the meeting is supposed to achieve – whether it is to vet the person's abilities or skills, to check their time availability, to see what their expectations of their involvement is, or to assess their reliability.

Remember, a volunteer who is very unreliable or has no free time is of little use to the group.

Volunteer Forms

It's a good idea to get volunteers to fill out a volunteer form, which you can then keep on file. Ask them to write their name, address and contact phone numbers (work and home), and the time they can give to the campaign. Include a list of tasks and/or sub-committees, and ask them to mark which they are interested in. You might leave a space for any particular skills or experience which they feel might be relevant and any personal contacts that might be of use, such as well-known people who could act as patrons, contacts in the media and relevant experts.

Depending on the nature of your campaign, you may also want to ask them for the names of two referees, who can provide a character reference on request.

Volunteer Packs

As new volunteers join up, it's a good idea to give them each a Volunteer Pack, which could contain

- leaflets and any other informational material.

- a short history of the campaign, highlighting any important developments or events.

- a list of names and contact numbers, including Committee members and, most importantly, the person responsible for volunteer support and co-ordination.

- any free promotional material, such as car stickers, badges, or posters, and a list of what is available for sale.

Training

Induction

An induction, or introductory, meeting is a very good way of welcoming new volunteers, and it provides them with important information relating to the campaign. It gives them an opportunity to meet and get to know members of the group, especially the Volunteer Co-ordinator, as well as other new volunteers. It is a good time to explain the do's and don'ts of the group, and any relevant procedures.

You may want to hold introductory meetings at regular intervals to cater for new members as they become involved.

Training Courses or Workshops

If you feel that your issue is complex, or you want to bring particular skills in the group up to a certain level, you may feel it is useful to organise some kind of training. If so, you will need to decide the following:-

- The purpose – You may want to organise training around the issues of the campaign or to improve people's campaigning or administrative skills.

- The content – What topics will you cover in each session?

- The time period – Will you run the sessions at weekends, or on week nights? How long will each be?

- Who will organise the training – This will entail booking the venue, arranging speakers and maybe buying refreshments.

- Who will lead the training and facilitate the meetings?

Confidentiality

For some campaigns, and for individual parts of others, being careful with information is a necessity. Getting this across to people at all levels of the group is important. It can be done as part of the induction process, part of formal training, or just communicated through the attitudes to confidentiality of the committee members.

While there is no need to become paranoid about 'spies in the camp', or tapped phones, there's probably no harm in being careful about what you say and where you say it, particularly if your campaign is raising hackles in powerful places. Be sparing with your information on the phone especially if it is a mobile, and be sure you trust the people who are let in on any of the more sensitive issues relating to the campaign. Even if the person does not mean to spill the beans, a careless word in passing can do a lot of damage. Always be careful about what you write down, as something in writing is much more likely to end up on an unfriendly person's desk or under the eye of a keen journalist.

Volunteer Management

When volunteers join the group it is a good idea to encourage them to be realistic about what they can offer the campaign.

People tend to function in one of two ways in groups. Some have the time and the energy to work in short, concentrated bursts, maybe getting involved for six weeks or so, perhaps returning at intervals after that. These people could focus on short-term or once-off activities, such as organising a protest or a fund-raising event. Others prefer to stay in for the long haul, building up their involvement as time goes by. They could be given more long term responsibilities, such as being a link person for a group of local volunteers.

The exact task given to a volunteer will depend on their interests and capabilities. People who are good at organising and co-ordinating could be given a lot of responsibility even if it is just for one event.

On a practical level, particularly at the beginning stages when you don't know your volunteers too well, it's a good idea to be very clear at meetings what tasks need to be done before the next meeting, and who is to do them. Leaving with a *check list* of what they have to do makes it easier for people to follow through. It is also very clear to everyone how and when things will get done.

When Volunteers Move on

Volunteers often come for a while and then drop out for various reasons – hopefully not because they are fed up! If someone has not turned up for a while, or seems uninterested, it's worth asking them why. This could turn up problems within the group which you might not otherwise discover.

Volunteers who no longer have the time or inclination to be involved directly with the campaign could stay in contact by going on the supporters list.

Supporters

Some people are supportive of your campaign, but won't want, or have the time, to become active volunteers. However, they may be very willing to give donations, to turn up at public meetings or marches, and to pass the word around amongst their friends and colleagues.

These people are a resource which is sometimes neglected by campaign groups. Build up a list of their names, addresses and phone numbers. Send them any newsletters or new leaflets, and keep them informed of forthcoming events, and fund-raising drives.

Some of these people might become volunteers at a later stage in the campaign.

CAMPAIGN CO-ORDINATOR

Role

Effective co-ordination, that is, the pulling together of all the strands and activities of the campaign as well as the needs of the campaigners, is crucial to its success. This is probably best achieved by having a Campaign Co-ordinator.

Functions of a Campaign Co-ordinator:–

- Overseeing the day-to-day running of the campaign.

- Managing the office and administrative work.

- Co-ordinating and supporting volunteers.

- Making sure that people fulfil their roles and responsibilities.

- Ensuring that the structures and procedures of the group are adhered to.

- Maintaining good channels of communication.

- Preventing or dealing with interpersonal conflicts.

However, if the group is very small you may not need a Co-ordinator as these functions are probably already covered by your Committee, or your Chairperson alone fulfils that role. Groups might also shy away from having a Co-ordinator if they feel that it would invest too much responsibility in one person. The concern here might be that the campaign would fall apart if that person were sick or on holidays.

Skills of an Effective Co-ordinator

Basically, a Co-ordinator needs to be a Jack or Jill of all trades, with plenty of enthusiasm, commitment, and patience, with a relaxed and open manner and a good sense of humour! They also need to be:-

- An efficient organiser and manager.

- A good leader, who leads and guides from behind, encouraging others to take responsibility. They do not need to be the 'brains' of the group, but rather an enabler who makes sure that the valuable input of others is put to good use.

- Able to communicate with people of all types and be sensitive to their needs.

- Good at making sure that everyone does what they have promised to do without being bossy, judgemental or condescending.

- A good mediator, who can prevent interpersonal fighting, as well as help to solve personal disagreements when they occur.

- Able to enthuse and empower others, particularly when things are not looking too hopeful.

- Aware of their own needs and limits.

- Able to remain calm, even when hit with the most unexpected crises.

- Prepared to do all sorts of work, sometimes doing boring jobs rather than always dumping them on others.

EMPLOYING PEOPLE

You may decide that you will take on a paid co-ordinator, or someone to help with office work. If your campaign is quite big, you may be in a position to employ a number of people.

Some Reasons for Deciding to Employ People

- There may be too much work and responsibility for group members to handle on a voluntary basis.

- The campaign needs to be managed on a full-time basis particularly during work hours.

- You want to introduce certain skills and experience into the group.

- You want to develop and expand the campaign.

- You want to give a professional image to the campaign.

Implications and Responsibilities of Being an Employer

- You will need to raise the money required to pay the wages (but often a good worker can help to raise more money) – never forget that when you employ someone you are committing yourselves to paying them as promised.

- You should work out a 'redundancy' package with the worker, so that they know what will happen to them financially if the campaign ends suddenly (which is bound to happen when you win!) and they are no longer needed. The main reason for doing this is to reassure the worker that they will not be dumped at the end without a little money to tide them over while they look for another job.

- It's best to put in place a clear disciplinary and grievance procedure at an early stage, in case problems arise with the worker in the future.

- Unless you are paying someone by contract and they are dealing with their own tax bill, you may have to register as an Employer and pay Employers' PRSI and PAYE. This will involve a fair amount of paperwork.

- Employing people can quicken the pace of the campaign. Often, rather than cutting down volunteers' workloads, this can increase the time commitment required by everyone – you need to be sure that you are ready for that.

Defining the Role and Accountability of the Worker

Prepare a job description, outlining the tasks to be done, the skills and experience you are looking for, the hours of work and where the worker will be based.

Be clear on who the worker is accountable to, who will provide support and supervision, and where they fit into the decision-making structure. Will they have voting rights? What meetings should they attend? Will you arrange regular review sessions? Do you want them to produce regular work reports? How will the worker's role relate to that of the volunteers?

The above may seem very formal, particularly if you are a small group employing someone you know, on a basis of mutual trust. However, later in the campaign your worker may change, or you may decide to increase the workforce. Therefore, it is best to pre-empt any problems which may occur, particularly in relation to possible power struggles and loss of control, by getting it right from the beginning.

Selection

As a number of people may be keen to take on the post from within your group, or members may be proposing their friends, you will want to be sure that the selection procedure is fair.

- Advertise the position through the media, or pass the word around locally through appropriate channels.

- Invite people to apply for the post by a certain date, enclosing a copy of their C.V. and the names of two referees.

- If a lot of people apply, draw up a shortlist of those who you feel should be interviewed.

- Decide on an interviewing panel (usually two or three members of your Committee, and perhaps also an objective outsider, who has experience of interviewing).

- Be clear on what you want to ask the interviewee. Asking open ended questions to allow them to elaborate as they see fit.

- Let them know when you will be making your decision.

Training

Good training is always an investment in the future, as the group should benefit from the trainee's new skills.

All workers, like volunteers, should attend any induction courses or training sessions organised by your group.

You may feel that the worker will need some further coaching in a specific area. If your budget allows, try to find an appropriate course and send them on it.

Fás Work Schemes

A number of schemes exist, whereby people are paid by FÁS to work in voluntary organisations. As well as providing paid staff,

---

Warning! – because of the nature of schemes, their length, the rates of pay, the qualifying restrictions (workers must be on Unemployment Benefit for a certain length of time, or signing on for Unemployment Assistance), you may find it hard to get people with the skills you are looking for, or they may leave once a full-time position appears elsewhere.

these schemes also provide grants towards administration costs. To find out what is available and whether you will qualify as an employer, contact your local FÁS office.

PEOPLE ISSUES

Support

Just as the joists in a building need each other to hold the structure together, the volunteers and workers in a campaign require each other's support.

Why support is necessary

A supportive group is one which provides good backing, encouragement, protection and friendship to all its members. People feel good being part of the group. They feel confident in their role rather than undermined, they fit securely into a well-managed structure rather than floundering in a stressful vacuum. They know that if things go wrong someone will be there to laugh it over with afterwards, or to help pick up the pieces. Support is not just something which the organising Committee has to provide for other members. It needs to be there for everyone.

Providing support is a key element for all voluntary organisations, but particularly so with campaign groups. Campaigns, by their very nature are unpredictable and often stressful. They bring together for an unknown length of time, a bunch of people, all of whom may be total strangers to each other with different views and personalities. While some may be seasoned campaigners, many will come into the group having little previous experience of campaign work. As well as not being used to the type of activities, they may find the unpredictability difficult to handle. When the campaign is not going so well, it will be hard not to feel demoralised. When it is on a roll, you may all become totally exhausted from sheer excitement and the amount of work.

Good support is necessary to make sure that people stay on track, that they all work together even during the difficult times. It helps to bond people together and prevent conflict.

Ways of providing support

- Create a supportive and friendly atmosphere.

- Communicate! Communicate! Communicate!

- Try to ensure that new volunteers and/or workers are introduced around and made feel welcome.

- Be sure that all volunteers know to whom they are responsible and to whom they can go for help or advice.

- Be sure to have space in meetings for people to air any difficulties they have come across during their campaign work. As some people may not like bringing up their problems, it is a good idea to regularly check out how they are getting along.

- Keep an eye on things, so that any practical or interpersonal problems that may emerge don't get out of hand.

- Treat everyone with respect, and be appreciative of their contribution, no matter how small.

- Add a social dimension to activities; gather in the pub after a stint of petitioning; have a cup of tea after meetings; organise campaign parties.

- While there may be a structural hierarchy in the group, try not to set up a situation where the 'bosses' make all the decisions, and don't get their hands dirty, while the 'grunts' at the bottom get all the bum jobs. It's very encouraging to group members, and also an outward sign of true dedication, when your Committee members muck in where necessary.

Providing practical support – expenses

You will want to make sure that anyone can become involved, regardless of their financial circumstances. Therefore, it is important to be clear from the beginning that you will pay expenses, so that no-one has to be out of pocket.

Draw up a list of expenses which can be claimed so that everyone knows what is or isn't covered. This may include anything from travel and phone calls made at home, to heating and lighting costs. People should be re-imbursed for anything they buy, such as stamps, stationery, and materials for banners or placards.

Be clear on the procedures for claiming, who to go to, and when. Always ask for a receipt, or other appropriate financial record, to keep your book-keeper happy.

Obviously if people don't want reimbursement, and wish to give this as their financial contribution to the campaign, that's their choice, but don't expect this from everyone. Cover the expenses willingly. There is nothing worse than being made feel you are stingy when you ask for a refund. After all the donation of people's time is worth a fortune in itself.

Communication

It's really important that everyone knows what is happening in all parts of the campaign, that channels of communication exist between Committees and members, and that no one feels excluded through lack of information. Too often bad feelings emerge when people believe that no-one has even bothered to let them know about something. They can imagine that they are not needed or respected, that no-one likes them, or that they are being ousted for some reason. If such thoughts are reinforced by further non-communication, bitterness arises, which may then result in all sorts of conflict, and sometimes the loss of good members.

Likewise, if the Co-Ordinating Committee is not aware of what individuals on the ground are doing, more problems can arise. Activities could take place in an unco-ordinated way, with all the loss of potential and confusion which that would involve. *Communication must be a two-way thing.*

Ways of ensuring good communication

- Create a structure that ensures there is a constant exchange of information between the Committee, sub-groups and all members, and also clear routes through which all can have an input into decision-making. (See Chapter 2: Structure.)

- Keep those on the volunteer list up to date on all activities and relevant meetings.

- Send everyone regular updates, or produce a campaign newsletter.

- Arrange regular volunteer or sub-group meetings, and make sure that people know where and when they take place.

- Hold meetings where all members of the group get a chance to voice their opinions on, say, the direction of the campaign or its future activities.

Dealing with Apathy

People in the group can get discouraged when they are faced with a lack of progress or with external apathy.

You may get comments about how there's no point in bothering, how you'll never win anyway, how no-one will listen to you, how they don't care because the problem doesn't affect them. Others will agree with your cause, agree that something needs to be done, but will not be prepared to support or help out. This kind of attitude from the public can be projected into the group, with members beginning to lose interest and enthusiasm.

Remember:-

* *Believe in what you are doing.* If you need an injection of enthusiasm, look for it from others who are also committed to the cause, go to a conference, read an inspiring book, talk to others who are affected by the problem and let your anger at their situation re-kindle your fire.

* When you feel that no amount of persuading or canvassing will change people's attitudes, let go, accept that they are not yet able or ready to hear or understand the seriousness of your message. Don't take it personally or get angry.

* Be supportive of each other internally, so that even if the outside world seems uninterested you are able to keep each other's fighting spirits alive.

Dealing with Burn-out

Burn-out basically means that someone gets totally exhausted, loses enthusiasm, and cannot work properly, as a result of overwork and prolonged stress. It is very common amongst campaign workers and volunteers. They may even become quite physically and mentally ill if the situation is not addressed early enough.

How to avoid burn-out

* Don't let the campaign take over your life. Learn how to switch off and relax, keeping up interests outside of the campaign.

* Be sure to get plenty of support for yourself. At times, this may mean looking for it from within the group, talking to supportive friends, treating yourself to a massage, joining a support group, or maybe seeing a counsellor.

- Manage your time so that you are not always rushing around like a mad thing.

- Don't work all hours of the day and night. Learn when and how to say NO!

- Look after your health.

- Take holidays and breaks away from the phone or office.

Dealing with Conflict

Conflict is a natural part of human life and it arises from difference. Different people with differing views can give a campaign a wealth of opinion from which to encourage change. Usually when conflict arises and is openly dealt with, people are stimulated to think more creatively, to come up with alternative ideas, and a better plan of action arises. Conflict within a group, if dealt with properly, can lead to better understanding and more trust between members, largely because differences are brought out into the open.

However, it is important to distinguish between creative tension and disabling disagreement and where possible, to prevent the latter or at least deal with it effectively. When conflict gets out of hand, much energy will be spent on dealing with the fall-out and the personal hurt created. Conflict within a group can lead to the infamous split, which, if created out of bitterness can be extremely destructive to the overall aims of the campaign. Such splits can also affect those involved.

Ways of preventing conflict

As with everything, prevention is far better than cure. The potential for conflict can be greatly reduced by setting proper group structures and ground rules from the beginning of the campaign. As we have seen in the previous chapters, these should include establishing a clear vision and aims, setting up structures so that people feel included and have a say, providing on-going communication and support, and laying ground rules in relation, for instance, to punctuality, smoking and listening while others are talking.

Preventing conflict is generally not something that you need to do consciously. Instead, it is the logical result of looking after the other People Issues dealt with already in this section.

Some group members, particularly in community-based

campaigns, may be aware of the potential for conflict because of previous experience of working together, or from watching how such community-based initiatives have worked in the past. As is often the case, community politics may mean that people are trying to work together from entrenched positions. In this instance, it may be useful to actively encourage one or more 'outsiders', who have not previously been involved on any side, to join the group. This fresh energy should help to move the group away from local differences. Outsiders are also in a good position to bring in new ideas and, sometimes, to challenge internal problems without appearing to bear old grudges.

Guidelines for dealing with conflict

Provide good support structures

Sometimes the nature of the campaign issue will be linked to the level of conflict that the group experiences. Group members may feel very marginalised and so are fighting for recognition and respect in the outside world. They may be campaigning on a serious health issue, with members who themselves are in pain or facing possible death. The campaign could be attracting a lot of outside hostility.

These emotions can be projected into the group, and reflected in members' dealings with each other. A recognition of what is happening and efforts to respond supportively to people's needs can help to diffuse the situation.

Encourage honest communication

Conflict often emerges from hidden sources of irritation. Concealment is almost bred into us so that, out of politeness and sometimes a fear of upsetting the status quo, we stay quiet until whatever it is drives us mad and we explode. Encouraging honesty amongst group members will help them to speak their mind before the problem escalates.

It does not need to turn into an ongoing therapy session – having clear open communication is enough.

Keep problems within the group

It's important that problems are aired openly and worked on within the group. If things are discussed behind people's backs, the problem will become bigger, rumours will spread and the hurt and anger will grow. Dealing with serious problems internally also helps to minimise the amount of 'dirty washing' that gets out locally or, in serious cases, hits the media headlines.

Facing up to and solving problems internally will also help the cohesion of the group.

Put response procedures in place

In the planning stages of the group, work out clearly how you will respond if people don't follow through on their responsibilities. That way, any emerging conflict can be avoided because the group will have a procedure for responding effectively to it.

Confront difficulties before they become crisis situations

Catching conflict before it gets out of hand requires that you both identify and confront it as soon as possible. Depending on the situation, this could be done within a group meeting, or else the Co-ordinator and/or another group leader could broker a solution outside of a meeting. This may mean bringing together the main participants in the row, and listening to the various points of view, with the emphasis on trying to solve the problem, rather than defending particular stances or factions.

Bring in an outside facilitator

Using help from outside should not be seen as a group failure to deal with the problem. Rather, it should be incorporated as part of the group process, even in the absence of conflict. If facilitated review sessions are held regularly, all members of the group have a chance to reflect and air their views on the development of the campaign, and suggest changes in structure or strategy. A skilled facilitator will be able to help guide the session so that everyone feels included and people are honest in their communication with each other.

Take care in choosing your facilitator. Ask around, look for recommendations and try to end up with someone who feels right. Don't be put off by the cost – it will be money well spent in the long run.

Remove troublemakers

There are some people who join campaign groups for their own private reasons, whose only contribution to the group is negative. It might be that their way of relating to other people is causing major problems, or they might be hindering the group in other ways. In extreme cases they might be blatantly trying to wreck the group.

The potential such people have to cause disabling conflict means that sometimes the only solution is to remove them. It can be a difficult decision, and might seem like an admission of failure to solve the problems in any other way, but sometimes it must be done.

The Co-ordinating Committee should have worked out a means by which such people can be asked to leave. It is best to discuss how this decision is made and who does the 'telling' before the situation actually arises. That way, the matter can be dealt with as calmly and painlessly as possible.

Split!

Another extreme solution is the group split. Unfortunately there are times when this is the only way out of a downward spiral of conflict. It will only be effective when the setting up of another group is based on differing views on strategy, and the split can be seen as a positive step. A good example of this is where the 'off-shoot' wants to take a more radical stance than the original group.

A serious danger exists where the 'split' is a direct result of bitter in-fighting. Festering anger can often mean that both groups end up competing with each other, rather than focusing on the targets of the campaign. For this reason, splitting the group needs careful consideration.

SAMPLE VOLUNTEER SHEET

Name: _____

Address: _____

_____

_____

Tel: (h)_____(w)_____

Please tick the areas of work in which you would like to become involved:

SHARING INFORMATION – with friends/contacts ☐

DOOR-TO-DOOR CANVASSING ☐
– leaflet drops, petition signing, requesting donations, etc

FUND-RAISING ☐

ADMINISTRATION ☐

Would you be interested in attending a Public Demonstration?
yes ☐ no☐

Would you like to receive information on the campaign's progress?
yes ☐ no☐

If you can help in any other ways, or can offer special expertise, please give details below:

_____

_____

_____

_____

_____

_____

_____

SOME OF THE LESS PRODUCTIVE CHARACTERS TO BE FOUND LURKING AMONGST CAMPAIGNS

The Talker

Not the best person to be given any responsibility, but otherwise fairly harmless.

- Good at talking – not so good at doing.
- A member of many other Committees (rarely just a ground troop).
- Very vocal at meetings.
- Is 'terribly busy' when jobs need to be done, but manages to be free to turn up at events.
- Has strong opinions on what should happen.
- Wants to be part of any major decision-making.
- The sort of person whose input seems very useful, but if you actually sit down to work out what exactly they have done the list is short.

The Digressor

Keep this person in line. If this doesn't work, gag them!

- A demon at meetings, continually drifting off on tangents.
- Doesn't give up, even if the chair manages to keep a hold of the meeting, instead cornering the person sitting beside them and continuing to talk.
- Finds it hard to focus on the aims of the campaign and is always bringing up new problems and crises which 'must' be addressed.

The Depressive

Try to enthuse them – failing this, ignore them.

- Nothing is right with the campaign.
- 'We will never win, nobody will support us, we won't be able to collect the money, it'll surely rain, the media will never turn up, the gig will be a flop.'

The Worrier

While they might drive you mad, their fussing can encourage careful planning.

* Scared stiff that something awful will happen.

* Not prepared to take a risk.

* Terribly afraid of upsetting someone.

The Anarchist

Don't let them throw you too far off course.

* Arrives at meetings wearing dark glasses and leathers.

* Hates politicians.

* Is impatient with the niceties of the campaign – roll on the Revolution!

* Advocates direct action at all times, even before the campaign starts.

The Power-Monger

This person has great potential to annoy people and unbalance the campaign – keep them in check.

* Likes to boss people around.

* Is very likely to go off and do things without the knowledge or agreement of other Committee members.

* Likes to have a number of loyal followers who will back them up in the event of a dispute or confrontation.

* Is very argumentative at meetings.

* Doesn't like not getting their own way.

The Arch Bore

You know the one! Learn to jump in and politely bring the discussion back to base.

* Goes on a bit at meetings, but usually doesn't say very much of interest or relevance.

* Is always phoning you up to drone on about something.

The Chaotic One

There is probably not an organised bone in their body – it is best to pair them off with others when it comes to carrying out a task.

- Usually very willing but completely scatty.

- Always late for meetings.

- Always forgets to bring whatever needs to be brought.

- Turns up at the wrong place at the wrong time.

- Sends letters to the wrong addresses.

The Thief

Under no circumstances make them the Treasurer! If money is around, keep an eye on them.

- Very keen to help at fund-raising events.

- Always offers to take the money at the door or to run the raffle.

- Eager to please at all times.

The Egotist

Ask them to speak at any gatherings where heckling or rotten tomatoes are expected.

- Likes the sound of their own voice.

- Is always keen to be the spokesperson on TV or at public meetings.

- Usually has no patience with new volunteers, or people with little knowledge of the campaign.

- Is arrogant and condescending.

Above: Peace rally in Dublin, February 1996
Below: Crowds gather at Carnsore Point in 1978 to listen to representatives of organisations opposed to nuclear power.

Above: *Greenpeace Ireland action at the French Embassy, commemorating the 10th anniversary of the sinking of the Rainbow Warrior, July 1995.*

Above: A pageant organised in conjunction with the Fire Station Arts Studio, ICON and CAFÉ, as a creative response to the issue of drugs in the North Inner Dublin City Community, November 1996.
Below: Peace rally, Dublin 1996.

Above: Amnesty International Information Stand.
Below: Dublin Bay Action for Health protesting on Sandymount Strand in 1995 at the proposed siting of a medical waste incinerator in Ringsend.

Above: The Cavan Potholing Gang.

Below: AFRI famine walk in Mayo,1989.

Above: *The launch of the 1995 Europe Against AIDS summer campaign in the Potato Market, Limerick. The campaign was co-ordinated by The Red Ribbon Project.*
Below: *Members of the Center for Independent Living, Irish Wheelchair Association and the Commission on the Status of People with Disabilities, together with leaders and Personal Assistants from CIL Mayo, at a two-day action outside Dáil Éireann, calling for the setting-up of an Independent Living Fund, July 1996.*

Above: March organised by the Donegal Uranium Committee – to protest against uranium prospecting and mining in the Donegal area.

Left: Hetty the Hen – Compassion in World Farming (see chapter 6).

Left: Participants in a march to Dublin Castle, organised jointly by the East Timor Campaign and the Tibet Support Group, to highlight the occupation and attempted annihilation of East Timor by Indonesia and of Tibet by China, July 1996.

Below: Joe Dowling, one of Ireland's haemophiliacs infected with the HIV virus, on the political campaign trail with campaign workers, 1991.

4

HOW AND WHERE TO ACCESS RELEVANT INFORMATION

'If you steal from one author, it's plagiarism; if you steal from many, it's research.'

Wilson Mizner, American playwright.

'Truth exists; only lies are invented.'

Georges Braque, French painter.

INTRODUCTION

In an age when the flow of information has become a torrent, and data can be bounced around the world in seconds, the campaign groups who know how to find what they need will have a definite edge.

There are not many campaign groups who can achieve their aims by appealing to people's emotions alone, and backing up the group's message with hard facts is essential to success. The risk of using poorly researched information, and the possible consequences, such as detracting from the group's message and damaging their credibility, should encourage people to put serious efforts into their search for facts. At the same time, the exhilaration of digging up some crucial data, which might tip the balance in your favour, makes the search all worthwhile.

This chapter will begin with some guidelines for the information seeker, and then move on to a wide range of information sources. Some are tried and tested, such as your local library, while others are still evolving rapidly and are beginning to impact on campaigning, such as the Internet. This chapter doesn't aim to give you all the answers, but at the end of it you should be able to read the signposts and begin your hunt.

REASONS FOR SEEKING INFORMATION

Information is power. Assembling accurate information on the subject is one of the main routes to a successful campaign. Accurate information is the basis on which you will:-

- Formulate a campaign strategy.

- Refute the case put forward by the opposition.

- Prepare submissions to the authorities.

- Prepare leaflets, posters, press statements, reports and public presentations.

Information you gather can also be used to put together the following:-

- **Soundbites.** Collect data suitable for soundbites or newspaper quotes at an early stage, so as to have on hand, should the opportunity to use it arise.

- **Anecdotes.** Poignant and interesting little stories or case studies are quite useful and attractive to the media as ways of illustrating your campaign, and so are well worth seeking out.

- **'Dirt'.** Maybe you want to gather some negative intelligence on a target. This is something which could weaken their position – damaging the credibility of the 'Rogues' or undermining your 'Rivals'. This 'dirt' is something you may have to dig quite deeply for.

BEGINNING YOUR SEARCH

Having identified the sort of information which you require, and the use to which it will be put, you should be able to save time and effort in your search.

Select the sources which seem most likely to have what you want, or at least offer a good starting point. Use any contacts you have access to and try to cultivate new ones. Follow the trail through the various organisations and agencies until you get what you need.

Bear in mind that you can almost always get the information you require, although sometimes the search might take a little longer or be a bit more difficult than you had expected.

SOURCES OF INFORMATION

The sources of information available to a campaign are many and varied. The following is a broad overview of these sources, and it should help to point you in the right direction. Be sure to consider all options, as one which you might otherwise ignore could prove very fruitful.

Local Knowledge

Seek out the information at your own doorstep before you try anywhere else. It is possible that there is information, verbal, written or recorded, around your area, which could prove vital to your campaign.

Folk knowledge, information which is passed around by word of mouth, can sometimes prove quite useful as a pointer. It is common in an area where something dubious is going on for people to 'just know' what is happening. Remember to use such knowledge carefully, searching out facts to back it up. *The use of unsubstantiated information could land you or your group in the courts charged with slander or libel.*

Don't discount the idea of contacting the company, individual or campaign target itself. They may not be able to give you the exact information you're looking for, but you might pick up something new, which could be useful.

Have a look at this list of other possible local sources of information:-

- Locals who live or work in key areas
- Locals who are 'in the know'
- Walkers and early morning joggers
- Residents' organisations and other local groups
- Your children
- Former and current employees of 'Rogues' or 'Powers that Be'
- Construction workers
- Local clergy
- Shopkeepers
- Gardaí
- Local doctors

- School Principal or teachers
- Business contacts
- Your Community Council
- Local Authority departments
- Local political representatives – Councillors and TDs

Directories

Directories are a great starting point in the hunt for information. They contain details of a wide range of bodies and services, and should guide you towards those most valuable to your campaign.

In addition to being available for purchase, you will find many of these directories on the shelves of your local library. Some, such as *Kompass* and *Who Owns Whom*, may be found in the business section, while others will be in subject areas throughout the library.

The following are worth looking at:-

Directory of National Voluntary Organisations, Social Service Agencies and other useful Public Bodies

Compiled by The National Social Services Board (NSSB), this book offers a comprehensive guide to a wide variety of voluntary organisations, State agencies, Community Information Centres and Health Boards.

This directory gives basic information on the role and services of each organisation, with their contact address, telephone and fax numbers. The subject index allows easy access to over two hundred topics, and there is also a section devoted to other sources of information. Again this is subject divided and includes sources within Northern Ireland, the United Kingdom and the rest of Europe.

IPA Diary

The Irish Institute of Public Administration produces an appointments diary – *Administration Yearbook and Diary*. It contains a valuable Directory at the beginning which is updated annually.

There is a very good Local Administration section in the yearbook in which you can find comprehensive information on the make-up and role of your Local Authority, Health Board, Vocational Education Committees, Regional Harbour Authorities and Fisheries Boards.

This directory will give you a complete and up-to-date list of all national, European and local politicians. It also contains a list of contact numbers for all national and local media organisations.

Other areas covered include local, national and European political bodies; the diplomatic service; the civil service; state agencies; major business organisations and companies; financial institutions; the defence forces; trade unions; religious institutions and orders; education; arts and some voluntary bodies.

It is readily available to buy from most book shops around Christmas and can also be found in your local library.

Kompass Directory

This is a large trade directory which gives brief and basic information on literally thousands of companies. Through this you can find out, under different categories, the type of business or services carried out by a company, the number of employees, product areas covered, names of the directors, the company's location, its parent company and so on.

All of the county libraries will have a copy as will many of the smaller branch libraries.

Who Owns Whom

The name of this book is almost self explanatory in that you can use it to find out who owns a certain brand or company by looking up the name in the index. It also works in reverse enabling the researcher to choose a company and find out exactly whom or what it owns. It is produced in a number of volumes which cover different parts of the world.

This type of information could be vital when pursuing an individual or company you may have identified as a 'Rogue' or 'Powers that Be'.

Directory of Libraries and Information Services in Ireland

If you wish to gather some more data on the Library Service in Ireland, this Directory is well worth looking at. It will give all the details you may require on a specific library. As well as the names, addresses, telephone and fax numbers of individual county libraries, it also carries details on the smaller branches and the name of the chief librarian in each one.

Other information includes any special collections, details on books, periodicals, audio, video and other materials, equipment available for public use and information on lending facilities.

Libraries covering areas such as development, community work, health, education and the arts – to name just a few – are detailed in this directory.

Directory of Irish Archives

This is a good reference if you require information on the specialist libraries. It gives practical information on where the libraries are, the area of interest covered, their stock of books, other resources and accessibility. It covers libraries that many members of the public may not have known even existed.

Similar in structure and layout to the *Directory of Libraries and Information Services*, it includes information on the Garda Síochána Library, the Irish Architectural Archive, the Central Statistics Office Archives and the RTÉ Archives, to name but a few.

The Local Library

Libraries may have a bit of a fuddy-duddy image, being associated with rows and rows of dusty, book-filled shelves. In the library of today, this is no longer the case where, as well as the old reliable printed matter, we can now find a full range of audio and video resources, computer databases and more recently, access to the Internet.

Individual county libraries and their smaller branches are funded by the relevant Local Authority to provide a comprehensive information service for the people of that county. The library service is something everyone in Ireland has direct access to, yet it is still an under-used information resource.

As many of the existing libraries are on-line, having computer access to the contents of other libraries throughout the country, a lender can receive a publication from their local library via the central, county and sometimes even larger libraries. So if what you're looking for isn't available in your nearest outlet, don't hesitate in asking the librarian. Using the network of Local Authority libraries throughout the country, your local library may access information from any branch in Ireland, regardless of where you live. Mobile libraries can also deliver on this but you'll probably have to wait until it next visits your area – usually every two weeks or so.

Keywording

Keywording is an easy reference method available in almost all libraries. The name of each publication will be stored on computer under a number of 'key words', based on its contents. This allows you to access books, reports and articles which may be relevant to your campaign by giving the librarian a number of words you would expect to find in the information you're looking for. They will use these words to call up a list of relevant publications, available in that particular library or in one of the other branches throughout the country.

For instance, a campaign group looking for information on divorce might try the keywords 'Divorce', 'Marriage', 'Separation' or 'Annulment'.

Reference Section

The reference section is where material is kept just for reference. You may not remove these books, but libraries with this facility will have space set aside for study.

In this section, you will find a selection of books on a wide variety of areas. Specialist topics such as science, technology, health, the arts, environment, religion and development issues are covered here.

Two important divisions of the reference area are the Business and Local History sections.

Business Section

Don't let the name put you off. There's a lot more to the Business area than you might think and it is a part of the library many of you will end up visiting at some stage or other.

As its name suggests, this section will have books, reports, periodicals and directories on all aspects of business as well as on individual companies. Some of the larger libraries will also have news clipping files on most of the better known names in business.

This is where you will find general information on legal matters, legislation, management, communications and so on. You will also find a selection of government publications, reports on a wide variety of topics, planning details, periodicals, trade journals, specialist magazines, subject divided news clippings and sometimes a selection of foreign news articles and papers.

Local History Section

The Local History area within the Reference Section is the place to go for information on individual County Council meetings. If you want to know what your local Councillors decided, have a look through the regularly updated minutes of all of the Council meetings over recent years, which you will find here.

In this area you can also find information on your local TDs and County Councillors – including contact names and addresses and clinic opening hours; the voters' register; local phone and business directories as well as published material on the general history of your area.

The library and modern technology

These days, institutions of all kinds, including the library are learning to adapt to, and use, the latest in computer technology.

ENFO Database

Almost all libraries now have access to the ENFO Database via computer and modem. ENFO is the Department of the Environment's information service (see later).

The information seeker can tap into an index of the resources of the ENFO library in Dublin, allowing you to identify publications and articles which might be of use to you. A copy of an article can be requested from ENFO, who will then post it to you.

As well as covering articles of Irish and European interest, this database includes a large listing from the US Environment Protection Agency (EPA).

Local Authority link-ups

In the future, you will be able to access a lot of Local Authority information from a computer database within the library. So, instead of going to the Local Authority's planning office for information on planning regulations or new applications, you can look up the data on the computer.

Access to the Internet

A growing number of libraries are now offering public access to the Internet (see later). Library customers can avail of this service free of charge and it is open to everyone.

You may need to book your time in advance.

Special Libraries

Copyright libraries

You may know the type of information you require, and even which book will give it to you but neither you nor your library can find it within the library network.

If the book in question was published in Ireland, you'll be able to find it in one of the copyright libraries that are scattered throughout the country.

Within one month of publication, a publisher must deliver a copy of any book which has been published in Ireland to each copyright library. These collections are to be found in the Academic libraries of the country's seven University Colleges as well as in the Acquisitions section of the National Library of Ireland.

Specialist libraries

A large number of institutions and agencies have their own private collection of books, reports and directories which are mainly for the use of their own staff in their day-to-day work. Many of these, however, allow limited access to the public, usually subject to appointment, constraints on space and limited opening hours.

- The Combat Poverty Agency's Library has information on areas as diverse as homelessness, transport, old age, unemployment, arts, disability and poverty.

- The National Social Services Board's Library has information on all aspects of the social and voluntary services, citizens' advice, voluntary sector funding, community work, social policy and much more.

- APSO, The Agency for Personal Services Overseas, houses a resource centre which has a comprehensive collection of information on the developing world.

- Trócaire, the Catholic Agency for World Development, has a small, yet well equipped library at the organisation's headquarters. This has a comprehensive stock covering topics such as justice, history, peace, economics, health, rural development, religion, environment, politics and economic policy, within the context of the developing world.

Other specialist libraries include The Central Catholic Library, The Law Library, The Irish Architectural Archive and the German Institute Library. Have a look through the Directory of Library and

Information Services in Ireland for more detailed information on those which might be relevant to your work.

ENFO

More than just a library, ENFO, the information service of the Department of the Environment, is an environmental information, resource and exhibition centre. Here, you'll find information on all aspects of environmentalism, conservation, preservation, ecology and other related topics.

Facilities include a well equipped library with an extensive stock of books, audio, video and CD-ROM material; access to the ENFO database allowing entry into an index of thousands of environment related articles; extensive free leaflets; video booths and a meeting room.

If you cannot make it into the library itself, you can phone in your request and the relevant information will be sent on to you, usually free of charge.

University/Academic libraries

You may wish to visit an academic library for particular specialist information, on, for instance, some geological, legal or management matter. Because most academic libraries are located in universities, and are regarded as being primarily for the use of the students, access may not be readily available.

Contact whichever library you want to visit, well in advance to find out about any restrictions which may be in place there – it's usually easier to get into an academic library at weekends or during holiday periods when the student demand is lower.

Newspaper Archives

Local or National Newspapers usually have a full archive of past editions of their paper. The number of back issues held by each office can vary depending on the age of the paper and the facilities available. Most archives are now available on microfilm or microfiche, which allows a large volume of news to be stored in a small space.

County libraries will also have back issues of the local newspapers on either paper or microfiche.

The Internet

The Internet is an international computer network, the core of which consists of computers permanently linked by high speed connections. To join in, all you have to do is connect your computer to any one of these. Once you are on-line (connected) your computer can talk to every other computer on the Internet, whether they are in your home town or on the other side of the world.

Having the Internet at your disposal allows you to find answers to many questions, send messages across the world instantly by E-mail, transfer documents, read the latest news in almost any language and link up with people with similar interests and concerns.

Getting On-line

You may already be able to access the Internet through work, college, school or your local library. A recent development is the CyberCafe, where access to the Internet is one of the items on the menu!

To get your own computer on-line, you need a modem, a phone line and an Internet connection. The connection is supplied by an Internet Service Provider, or ISP. ISPs are commercial organisations which allow you, for a fee, to connect your computer to their computer, which is permanently connected to the Internet.

The other cost will be your phone bill, but ISPs like Ireland On-line have points of presence (access points) around the country, so that your charges will be at local rates.

Companies' Registration Office

Situated in Dublin Castle, the office of the Companies' Registrar holds business information on all companies registered in Ireland. Here, for a charge (£1.50 – £3), you can access information about a particular company. This consists of financial information, details of shareholders and directors, and the company's Memorandum and Articles of Association.

You can also request specific information by post. Add £1 to the cost for postage and packing.

GOVERNMENT INFORMATION

Government Press Office/Information Service

By contacting this office, you can access basic information on the Dáil, Seanad and government make-up. A series of fact sheets which covers the role of the Oireachtas, its activities and services, is available on request. Unusual queries in relation to both houses should be addressed to this office which, if it cannot assist, will point you in the right direction.

Government Publications Office

This is the central source of all of the latest government reports and surveys and also contains an archive of older publications. There is a charge, sometimes quite substantial, for these publications, so you might prefer to search your library first. A number of government publications should be available in the reference section.

Other Useful Government Sources

Individual Government departments hold a wide range of information, and with the development of legislation on this matter it should be easier to get what you require from them.

The Central Statistics Office, EOLAS and The Environment Protection Agency might also prove helpful.

EU Information

In relation to EU matters, you can contact the Irish office of the European Commission for details on their work. Information on MEPs is available from the European Parliament office.

ACCESS TO INFORMATION ON THE ENVIRONMENT REGULATIONS

The 1996 Access to Information on the Environment Regulations, which replace the 1993 Regulations, state that information relating to the environment and held by a public authority, must be made available to anyone who requests it.

This covers written, audio, visual and database information and applies to any available information on the state of the natural environment and on anything which is likely to affect or protect it.

Environment related information carried or stored by any public authority, Government Departments, semi-state bodies, Local Authorities or any persons acting for these is covered under this regulation.

There are certain exceptions, however. Environmental information relating to national or international defense or security, commercial confidentiality or matters which are sub-judice, is not covered under this regulation.

More detailed information on the Freedom of Access to information on the Environment Regulations is available from ENFO.

HOW TO FIND WHAT YOU WANT ON THE INTERNET

With the wealth of information on the Internet, you may find it a bit daunting at first. However, help is at hand:-

Search Engines

These are on-line databases (or groupings of files) that constantly collect and index information about what is on the Internet. Just as you would search through a database on a computer in a library by author or subject, so too would you use a Search Engine to find what you want on the Internet.

You do not need to be a computer programmer, as the graphical interface of the World Wide Web, the WWW, makes it all as easy as clicking your mouse button.

The bottom line is that much of the information which a campaign group might require can be accessed by a few simple Key Words. Once you are in the right area you will be guided towards other related pages, and who knows what you might turn up!

Further Help

If that is not enough, there is a whole range of books and magazines about the Internet and how to find information on it.

Still, there is nothing to stop you diving straight in, and then looking for help once you get there. Before you go in search of specific information, you should learn to find your way around the 'Net. There are special newsgroups for newcomers, just to help you out. You will also find a section of Frequently Asked Questions, or FAQs, so you will probably get the answers you are looking for without even having to ask.

The Internet is essentially a global community using the technology for communication. It has a rich tradition of helping out visitors and newcomers. So, when you connect, don't be afraid to ask for help – you might be surprised at how many people will direct you around the 'Net.

ANECDOTE: RED RIBBON PROJECT

The **Red Ribbon Project***, formerly known as the Limerick AIDS
Alliance, provides HIV prevention and support services within the
mid-Western region. Much of their work involves the co-ordination
of awareness-raising campaigns.*

Making the most of information gathered, the **Red Ribbon Project**
whilst co-ordinating The Europe Against Aids Campaign in
Ireland turned it to their full advantage. The summer campaign
was getting only marginal publicity yet there were over twenty
European countries involved. After attending the REM concert at
Slane, the Red Ribbon Project discovered that this was an ideal
situation for the dissemination of information.

Outreach workers were asked if it was easier for a girl or a guy to
get HIV? Can HIV pass through a condom? Can you get HIV from
a cut and what are vaginal fluids? Young people were telling the
outreach workers that they were not getting information on
HIV/AIDS at school, nor was the subject being discussed at home.
One young person said that he would rather spend money on hot
dogs than on condoms! All in all the feedback was worrying. So we
decided to capitalise on this and use the information in our press
release for FEILE.

The result was astounding. The media, print and broadcast,
national and local all picked up the release and AIDS and condoms
were discussed in the public forum. The campaign became known
and it increased interest when the minibus attended other events
locally.

We have learned to listen to people, to use the information
anonymously if it contributes to increasing awareness. Keeping an
ear to the ground can indeed be the best source of valuable
information.

Mairead Lyons, Co-ordinator.

5
FUND-RAISING

'Every one that asketh receiveth, and he that seeketh findeth.'
St Matthew 7. 8.

INTRODUCTION

Almost every campaign requires money to sustain it. For most, the ability to raise funds determines the potential for success. For this reason it is essential to have a positive and planned approach to fund-raising.

The campaign will determine which form of fund-raising is appropriate. Getting it right means the difference between the constant headache of trying to make ends meet, and the freedom to put the maximum effort into what your campaign is really about.

This chapter aims to get you thinking about *the appropriate approach for your group*, and to put forward a wide range of fund-raising methods.

CAMPAIGN TYPE

A big influence on the difficulty, or ease, with which you can access money will be the type of campaign you are working on. It is worth bearing this in mind when putting together a fund-raising plan, although many people will know intuitively what will and will not work for their group. Looking at your group in terms of the categories we suggested in Chapter 1: Planning, might help further in identifying your starting point for your fund-raising efforts.

An important point here, which affects more than just fund-raising, is *the way you present your message*. Some campaigns, such as unpopular and reactive ones, would benefit from stating their aims in positive rather than negative terms. This kind of positive image should improve access to funds.

Other avenues worth considering when you find that your campaign type seems to be limiting your potential for fund-raising include seeking out national bodies with similar concerns and looking beyond our own shores for assistance. Consider fund-raising events like pub quizzes, concerts and discos, which often attracts participants irrespective of the cause.

ORGANISATION

Having one person or a sub-group fully responsible for fund-raising is desirable. The benefit of this comes from the clear definition of who should arrange what, and from acknowledging the importance of fund-raising as a necessity.

Looking at it in broader terms, every member of the campaign who wants to see it succeed must throw in their bit of thought and effort when required. It is important to realize that the fund-raising group is responsible for seeing that the funds are brought in, but that does not mean that they must do it all themselves. Giving a person the title of fund-raiser does not absolve the group from their responsibilities in this regard.

As with other aspects of campaigning, advance planning will pay off. Fund-raising must be an integral part of the overall plan for achieving campaign goals, and the fund-raising committee should work closely with other functions.

To begin with, take a look at the activities set out in the Action Plan and the corresponding budget. This will show what funds are required, and when they are needed. Once the committee has its financial targets, it can set about studying the campaign plan for income opportunities. This process should become established practice, with consideration of fund-raising potential at the development stage of all campaign events.

From this the fund-raising group can begin to build up its own timetable of events – the Fund-raising Plan. Based on expected income, gaps will appear where overall targets are not being met, and further fund-raising methods must be considered. Once these further activities are penned in, the timetable will serve as the basis for sourcing finance during the planning period.

It is seldom difficult to draw up the plan. What is essential is that it contains projects which suit the campaign and the group's composition, and which will produce a good return for effort. Advice at this point, from someone with good fund-raising experience, can be beneficial.

Maybe the 'Campaign in a Perfect World' could sit back at this stage and everything would go according to plan, but for the rest of us the reality is that things seldom work out like this. Unforeseen expenses and changing events in the campaign will constantly knock your budget off track, and the fund-raising group must be quick to respond to such setbacks. Equally, unexpected income opportunities can present themselves, and a swift response from the committee could save time and effort later.

FINDING THE 'FUN' IN FUND-RAISING

Far too often seen as an unpleasant necessity to be put off as long as possible or passed on to somebody else, fund-raising is packed with the potential to involve more people, build teamwork, develop links with other groups, spread the campaign message and even have fun!

If your group holds the dreary image of fund-raising, then get rid of it now. Realise that you will have to get money in and having a long face won't change that. Instead see it as a challenge, an outlet for creativity and an opportunity for some entertainment.

Remember that whatever you are about to try has probably been done already by somebody else in the area. Ask them how they got on, and learn from their mistakes. Who knows, maybe they would like to help out, or maybe even another group might like to share the organising and the income. Pooling efforts like this will make for a stronger campaign movement in general and save you from falling into the same old holes.

Get more people involved. You won't do this by whinging about all the money that needs to be raised, so circulate some new ideas and make it interesting. Teenagers and children are likely to be a fount of ideas for types of sponsored event, and their energy can be infectious. Encourage them to join in and be willing to listen and even let them get on and organise events themselves.

Then there's the fun. A group financed solely by government grants would miss out on a whole range of activities which help to develop the co-ordination and cohesion within the group. They would miss the satisfaction that comes from emptying a collection box on the table to count, the pleasure in handing out raffle and spot prizes, and the *craic* of so many of the social activity fund-raising events like quizzes and gigs.

Face it, you have to fund-raise, so why not enjoy it?

CENTRAL FUNDING

Because of the diversity of campaign groups, it is hard to make generalisations, but it is probably fair to say that institutional funding is not a significant source of income for most.

While campaign groups are usually 'calling for' something to be done, or not to be done, most institutional funding of the voluntary sector is aimed at groups who are actually providing a service themselves. Groups need to see which of their activities would bring them into that category, maybe educational work for example, and use that as a basis for such applications.

Any group considering looking for funds from the following sources should get a copy of *The Irish Funding Handbook*. This book gives a directory of grant making trusts, European Union programmes, and the statutory and corporate sectors in Ireland, both North and South. It also advises on putting together applications.

Central Government

Funding for campaign groups might be available through a number of Government Departments, such as Environment and Social Welfare, the regional Health Boards, and National Lottery.

Some of these schemes are advertised in the national papers, so keep an eye out for them. Others supply funding to voluntary groups on an ongoing basis, and should be contacted for details about types of projects funded and application procedures. Your chances of receiving finance from any of these sources will depend a lot on your campaign, but you should at least check out the funding criteria of any which are relevant to your group before discounting them.

In applying for funding, first make the application, and then follow it up with requests for a meeting to go over it. It seems that more grants are allocated to groups who lobby.

Local Authorities

The chance of getting funding for a campaign group from your Local Authority is quite slim. Funds available are usually aimed at community groups carrying out activities in the areas of Arts and Community Development.

Due to the variation from place to place, it is best to contact your Local Authority directly, find out what funding is available, what the criteria for applicants are, and see where those funds have been allocated in recent years.

European Union

Equally unlikely to be of assistance for campaign groups are the various funding programmes of the European Union.

The process of identifying a suitable program and submitting an application is likely to take as much time and effort as your campaign work, and may not be worth the effort in the end.

It is much more likely that some level of awareness of EU funding could be used as a campaign tool. Lack of resources is a regular excuse from the target of campaigns, from both 'Rogues' and 'Powers that Be', as they explain how they could not possibly meet campaign demands. Being able to point them in the direction of finance which they were reluctant to seek could be a useful move in the campaign.

Other Institutions

Corporate sponsorship, as distinct from corporate donations, is a mutually beneficial setup. In return for supplying your campaign with money, goods, or even services such as office space or a PR person, they get their name associated with your group, usually in some very public way. Your chance of getting assistance is higher where there is a tie-in between the campaign objectives and the interests of the potential sponsor.

Naturally it is only publicly acceptable campaigns that need bother applying for this kind of assistance. (See Warning! at the end of this chapter.)

In approaching a company, remember that they will want to see the benefits to them from any proposed deal, and make these clear in your proposal.

Grant giving trusts fund a wide variety of community initiatives, but again there is more money available for groups that are 'doing' rather those which are 'campaigning'.

For full details of trusts in Ireland, refer to *The Irish Funding Handbook*.

FUNDING FROM THE PUBLIC

The suitability to your group of each option mentioned below will depend on various factors such as the number of people available to help and the size of the local community. Don't rule out any method without giving it some thought and looking at ways of adapting it to your situation.

Money on Demand!

Street collection

The 'flag day' can be a good earner, especially for popular campaigns. The amount of organisation and work required can be significant, but it can be well worth the effort. Wearing identifying bibs makes the collectors more prominent and helps to promote the group's image. Having closed collection boxes, rather than open buckets, makes sure that what goes in stays in! Some form of banner, display, or music can act as a focal point and attract more attention. A recent development is the 'selling' of badges, such as The Irish Cancer Society's Daffodil Day. This involves extra costs, but then promotes itself by the public wearing the badges.

Door-to-door collection

This can be an opportunity to explain the group's message to people face-to-face, as well as getting in some funds. The addition of some attraction, such as carol singers, should bump up the income. If your collection is to include local pubs, be sure to get permission in advance.

In both of the above collections, it is important to plan and co-ordinate quite well to maximise the return. Collectors should be well briefed on the group and the campaign as they are going out as ambassadors. Also, they should carry identification to show that it is a permitted collection. (See Legal Considerations later.)

Appeal

The appeal could consist of appearances on the radio and in other media, and a leaflet drop in appropriate areas, giving an address or bank account to which to send donations. It can be effective when there is heightened public awareness or concern, brought about by your own campaigning or after a specific event or controversial documentary.

Big donations

A single large contribution from a local celebrity or business person is likely to give the highest return in relation to effort. Target especially anybody who might have major sympathy with the campaign. (Indeed, such people might become 'Patrons' – see Chapter 6: Promotion of the Group and Message.)

Fixed collection boxes

Normally placed near a cash register and fixed in place to prevent theft, a collection box usually invites people to part with their loose change. With most of the best spots already taken, some innovation is needed to find new locations and ensure a worthwhile return. An unusual or appealing design might make the box more noticeable, while combining collection box and leaflet dispenser could benefit both objectives.

Wages scheme

Where your campaign has almost universal support, workers in a local business might be willing to have a small deduction made from their pay packet each week, with the scheme being administered by the company. A small contribution from a large work-force could provide a regular income for the group. Such a scheme relies on a huge amount of goodwill, and is quite limited in its application.

Something for their Money

Cake or jam sale

Group members and friends prepare some homemade produce, especially cakes and buns and jams, and these are priced and sold at a local venue, the event being publicised well in advance. Outside a church on Sunday mornings works well. Be sure the food is good though!

Jumble

Get people in the area to contribute items which they no longer need, from garden tools to children's toys, maybe by a general appeal and then calling door-to-door. A central venue and good promotion should get the people in, and remember to reduce the prices towards the end to avoid being left with a pile of 'stuff'.

Car Boot Sale

Organise a venue, such as a field or car park. People who want to sell something from the boot of their car must pay an entry fee to set up their stall. The public can also be charged a smaller entry fee.

Auction

Here you are looking for a string of worthwhile donated goods or services, and a packed hall of bidders with money in their pockets. Items donated or signed by celebrities can fetch a good price.

Coin snake or tower

A public event where people are encouraged to add coins to a line on the ground with the aim of making a very long snake, or building them into a tower.

Sponsored events

Traditionally limited to walks and such like, there is almost no limit to the sort of thing that can be tried here. From swims and cycles to all kinds of sports' marathons, and from excesses of food and music to abstinences such as fasts and silence. It can be a completely fun event, such as pushing a bed around town, or downright exciting, such as a parachute or even a bungee jump. Sponsored events are well worth considering, and can be very lucrative.

School Fund-raising day

If you can get a local school involved, then there is a range of events which they could use to collect money, including 'No Uniform Day', sports marathons and film showings.

Pub or table quiz

This can be a fun night out and doesn't require too much by way of preparation. A venue that will draw a good crowd, a simple set of rules, and a set of not-too-difficult questions with the right answers is all that you need. After that, promote it like mad, and collect up a few spot prizes for the night to help round off the entertainment.

Raffle

Get the prizes and tickets, promote the draw, sell the tickets! This falls into two categories, based mainly on size. A small raffle is easy to manage, usually involves small prizes which are easy to lay hands on, tickets are cheap, and it is usually very short term. Raffles like this can be simply promoted through friends or maybe some local outlet, and one is easily tagged on to other events such as a play or concert, increasing the money taken at the event. The larger raffle has also gained some prominence, with specially printed tickets, large volume sales, higher ticket price, and substantial prizes such as major holidays.

Coffee mornings

A person plays host to some friends, supplying tea and biscuits and telling them a bit about the campaign, in return for donations.

Lottery

The success of the National Lottery has influenced the direct flow of funds to charities by soaking up 'spare' cash, but we can take a lesson from this and apply it to our own fund-raising efforts. The bottom line is that people seem to like a game of chance with the possibility of winning a cash sum, and a system which takes in more than it gives out makes money. Simple, eh? A good example of this is bingo. An even simpler system consists of a numbered grid on a sheet of cardboard, with people 'buying' a box and a cash prize of maybe half the takings going to the winning number. This kind of system could be run on a weekly basis in a local pub or community hall.

Give this one some thought and you could come up with something perfectly suited to your own campaign and which could provide a nice regular bit of income.

Concert/gig/céilí/ball/disco

Organising an event like this from scratch without experience could be a bit of a nightmare. If people are eager, and will take advice, then they should be able to pull it together, as energy and determination can achieve great things. However, convincing someone who normally promotes or organises such events to run a benefit for you is probably the best option, but the group will need to keep an eye on anything done in its name, as well as helping to promote the event.

Membership

Most national campaigning organizations have some form of membership base who pay a minimum amount each year, and in return receive a newsletter and further information about the campaign. By encouraging people to pay by standing order and maybe spreading payment over the year, the organisation has a fairly reliable source of income which enables it to budget well in advance.

This can also be applied locally, providing regular funds, a measure of support for your campaign and an audience to educate further through some form of news sheet.

Stall at open events

Where there are people, there are potential donors. A stall offers you the chance to communicate directly with people who may just have a passing interest in the campaign, or even be downright hostile. No stall would be complete without some element of fund-raising – a collection box at very least (well nailed down) and any other of your methods which seem appropriate such as membership forms, merchandise and maybe even a raffle. Stalls need to be okayed by event organisers, usually well in advance. *Setting up stalls in public places requires permission from the Gardaí.*

Merchandise

Campaign

It is part of modern popular culture to pay for the privilege of advertising for a company by wearing its name emblazoned across your chest on trendy clothing, and campaigning groups have learned well from this.

Selling group merchandise has a dual function – the promotion effect of people wearing your message on their T-shirts and bags, and displaying your stickers in their windows is considerable. A price needs to be set for such goodies which brings in some income but does not discourage widespread purchasing. This is one you will need to judge for yourself.

In having merchandise made up for you, try to give a little thought to the soundness of what you buy. For instance, if you were running a campaign on women's rights you wouldn't like to be selling clothes from a producer with a poor record in equality in the workplace, would you? Things like this happen all the time, but with a little effort it need not happen in your group.

Other

If you are selling items to the public, such as through a stall or from the campaign base, then it should be possible to find other products which might be appropriate to sell and get in a bit more cash. It would be best to stick to items related to your campaign and which might not be widely available elsewhere, such as a full recycled paper range for an environmental group or Fair Trade products from Fair Trade Éireann for a human rights or development group. Locally made crafts might also find a place here.

Legal considerations

A special permit is required from the Gardaí for any form of collection from the public, such as a street or door-to-door collection. This permit is also required for sponsored events. An application should be made to your local Garda Station, and the licence is then granted at the discretion of the Chief Superintendent for the area. Be sure to look for such permits well in advance.

A further requirement for collections, which is also common sense, is that boxes should be sealed while the collection is in progress.

Raffles come under a Lottery Permit, which can be granted by the local Superintendent through the Garda Station. The prize limit is set at £3,000, and only two draws can be made by a group in any one year.

A Lottery Licence can be granted by the District Court, and this covers a twelve month period. Under this licence a payout can be made every week, with the upper limit per week set at £10,000. This would cover the likes of weekly bingo, as well as major draws and prizes.

Stalls set up in public for selling merchandise will need a Casual Trading Licence, issued by the Department of Industry and Commerce, and might also require a Casual Trading Permit from the Local Authority.

If your fund-raising clearly comes under any of these restrictions, then you are obliged to get the correct permission. If you are in doubt about a certain proposed activity, check in at your local Garda Station where a sergeant can judge if you need some form of permit or not.

You might want to consider insuring some fund-raising activities, particularly if there is any degree of risk to participants. Get advice from your solicitor on this one.

Warning ! In accepting funding from any source, you are placing yourself in a sort of moral debt to them. If you receive regular funding from a single source then you may develop a reliance on it and further compromise your independence.

Where the source is the public, this is less of a problem, as the vast majority of campaign groups acknowledge their responsibility to society. The problems begin when we come to government funding of certain campaign types, and funding by business and industry. When you accept such funding you are possibly leaving yourself open to their influence, the degree being dictated partly by the amount of money. This influence can be self-imposed – for example altering an education project in order to qualify for a grant – or forced – such as a business sponsoring a booklet so long as certain comments in it are removed.

In considering taking money from a company, you should check to see if they are engaged in practices which are damaging to your cause. It is a common approach for large companies to make funds available to campaigning groups and buy themselves credibility, rather than tackle their problems in the area of workers' rights, pollution and so on. In such a case you must balance the urgency of the need for funds against improper sourcing.

BEYOND THE JOKE

'Beyond the Joke' *was a single issue campaign formed in 1994 in response to an attack on a young woman in a pub in Derry.*

When this woman objected to a man repeatedly making sexist comments to passing women, she was forced to the ground and her neck was slashed with a broken beer glass.

Quickly realising we needed money to run a poster campaign, we decided to run a disco. This was to be both a fund-raising and awareness raising event. We chose the venue of the assault because it was very popular, central and free.

Following much discussion, we settled on a women only policy. In retrospect, it would have been a better idea to ask men for a donation rather than encouraging them to buy a ticket to an event they were asked not to attend. The resulting discussions (and arguments!) took the focus away from women's right to a hassle-free social life.

Organising the event was made much easier by being able to base the campaign at Derry Women's Centre and having a volunteer there who put a lot of time into it. We used personal connections wherever possible. A friend was happy to do D.J. for free, another friend provided free photocopying and stamps, and so on. Most people were glad to help once specific suggestions were made to them.

Local businesses gave us raffle prizes. As well as being another fundraiser, the raffle gave us an opportunity to explain why we were running it.

Advertising was seen as central, both to get women to attend and to raise general awareness. Press statements were published by two local newspapers and the *Irish News*. We postered the city centre a few days beforehand.

Our logo, a woman with arm outstretched, also adorned a mural on the back of Free Derry Corner for a few weeks. Well positioned in terms of volume of passing trade, the vagueness of the slogan ('the joke's over lads') however combined with the wall usually displaying republican slogans with at least one person interpreting it as Nationalist Ireland rejecting the Downing Street Declaration!

We raised over £200, had a great night out and created debate for a few weeks before and after the actual event.

Helen Harris

6

PROMOTING THE GROUP AND MESSAGE

'It takes two to speak the truth – one to speak and another to hear.'
Henry David Thoreau, American writer.

INTRODUCTION

No matter how vital you think your campaign message is, if you cannot communicate it to people then you can expect to make slow progress.

The public is bombarded every day with ads, images and news, so you have to be cute to catch their attention.

The aim of this chapter is to give you an understanding of how you can present the various elements of your campaign in a co-ordinated and effective manner.

PRESENTING AN IMAGE

While you may not want to appear like you have been moulded by a PR company, the image you present to the public is hugely important to the campaign and its development. Obviously, what you say and how you say it will give people a good idea of the sort of a group you are, but building an image can entail a lot more than just working out the right words.

In this section, we will focus on other important elements, such as choosing your name and logo, working out campaign slogans, and gathering a list of patrons. Remember, being able to effectively create an image also sends out a message to the 'Powers-that-be' that you are an organised and professional group, a force to be reckoned with on all levels.

The first step to take is to sit down and work out what kind of image you actually wish to project. Do you want to come across as being positive rather than negative, radical or more middle-of-the road, caring and compassionate, or determined?

When you are considering this, it is worth bearing in mind *the importance of appearing constructive rather than destructive*. In the past, campaign groups used to get slated for being so negative, for always yelling 'No!', without suggesting any other options. While obviously in some cases there are no alternatives, and you are dead right to voice your definite 'No!', it is good from the beginning to make it clear what you feel should happen instead. This shows that your campaign has a solid vision. Likewise, try to avoid putting out a NIMBY (Not in My Back Yard) image. While you may be objecting to something in your area, you don't want people to think that you would be happy if it was just dumped somewhere else.

Your Group's Name

It's important to pick the right name, as it will be very difficult to change it once the campaign is launched. Your name will probably be the first link most people will have with your campaign.

Try to relate it to your chosen image. If focusing on the positive, choose a name with an optimistic ring to it, such as 'Action for Better Education'. If you want to make it obvious that you are very representative, try 'Coalition of ....', or 'Combined...'

Make sure that it rolls off the tongue easily. Often people think up a name because it sounds descriptive, but realise later that it is a complete mouthful, and a nightmare for anyone who has to answer the phone – 'Hello, Ballymaghahon and Glenamuck Action for Better Housing.'

Pick a name which says something about your group, but is short and catchy. Alternatively, try to end up with a relevant acronym, such as CRAP – 'Combined Residents Against Pollution.'

Once you have your name, you can always add an explanatory statement beside it. For instance, 'Combined Residents Against Pollution – Campaigning to Close Down Ringlawn Dump.'

To choose your name, you may want to hold a brainstorming session with all the group members, or maybe hold a competition locally. If nothing too exciting is emerging this way, you could always ask for suggestions from someone who works in advertising or marketing.

Campaign Slogans

While you're hunting around for a good name, you might as well work out a few good slogans which relate to the image and message of your campaign as well. These can be used on banners, placards, posters, leaflets, car stickers, beer mats. One may become the definitive slogan for the campaign – such as the Dublin Bay Action for Health Group's 'NO TO INCINERATION' Campaign.

Slogans can be hard-hitting or fun, the punchier the better. If there is a poet amongst you, try composing a few little ditties. As well as looking good on placards, these sound great when yelled through the megaphone at the front of marches. A rhyming dictionary is very useful for this, as is a thesaurus.

You could even go a step further and put together a campaign theme song, so long as it isn't too corny!

Campaign Logo

As soon as you come up with your campaign name, rope in a friendly graphic artist to design (hopefully free of charge) a suitable and eye-catching logo. This should illustrate the type of image you are trying to project, and should not be too complicated – you will want it to be recognised and understood at a glance. An effective logo is one which, over time, can stand on its own, one which people will automatically associate with your campaign.

Explain your desired image to the artist, and give them your campaign name and slogan. Ask them to sketch a few options and then choose the most suitable.

This logo can be printed on your letter-headed paper, leaflets and informational material, posters, T-shirts and any other merchandise.

Patrons and Supporting Organisations

A patron is a well-known person who lends their name in support of a particular group or project. Likewise, supporting organisations are groups who are willing to publicly endorse your campaign. A group's patrons and supporting groups are usually listed on their letter-headed paper, on leaflets and other informational material.

A good list can add credibility to your campaign image, particularly at the early stages when no-one knows too much about you – 'ah, it must be okay if so-and-so is supporting it.' Some patrons may be keen to offer financial aid, to help with fund-raising, or to introduce you to good contacts, while others may be willing to speak at events or to turn up for photocalls. Supporting organisations will be busy carrying out their own work, but may be able to give advice.

If this happens it's great, but don't forget that people in the spotlight are always being asked to donate their time or money, so don't expect too much from them. Getting permission to add their names as patrons can be valuable enough in itself. It is also quite a generous and trusting act on their behalf, as often they are associating their names with a new group, about which they may know very little.

Letter-headed Paper

Once you have your group name, logo and a list of patrons and supporting organisations, you should get your artist to design your letter-headed paper. Usually, the name and logo goes at the top, with patrons/supporting groups at either side or at the bottom.

If you feel that you won't need too many, the master copy can then be photocopied.

However it is better and probably more economical for most groups to get a few reams printed. If you decide to print in colour, make sure it is dark enough to come out well if photocopied. While more than one colour looks nice, it is much more expensive.

If you decide to use recycled paper put 'printed on recycled paper' at the bottom, just to make the point!

Banners and Placards

It is always good to have at least one large banner highlighting your group name or main campaign slogan. (See Chapter 8: Public Protests for further information on how to make these.) A clear banner at the front of your march leaves no one in any doubt as to who you are or what your message is. Banners can also be placed behind the speakers at press conferences or public meetings, or hung off relevant structures as part of a protest action.

Every campaign should also have a good selection of placards, for use at marches and rallies. A number of these in the same style can work very well in projecting the campaign image at such protests.

Other Promotional Material

Your group name, logo and campaign slogans can also be highlighted on other promotional material, such as car stickers, beer mats, badges, posters, T-shirts and sweat shirts, postcards or greeting cards. While you may want to make money out of these items, bear in mind their promotional importance when you set the price – it may be better to have more cars displaying your message, and more people wearing your T-shirts, more people receiving Christmas cards with your message on them, than actually making money. You may even decide to give them out free.

The Image Effect

Be aware of the strong image which can be created by getting people to wear the same T-shirts, or to dress in a certain colour at marches, photocalls or other public events. Wearing a campaign 'uniform' gives a clear sense of speaking with the one voice. It also looks great in photographs.

GETTING YOUR MESSAGE ACROSS THROUGH INFORMATION AND EDUCATION

Creating an image is one step, following it up with a well-organised information and education drive is the next obvious way of getting your message to policy-makers and the public alike. In this section we will look at how you can do this effectively – through the preparation of informational material, holding public meetings, running training courses and putting up information stands.

Leaflets

A good leaflet is often the cornerstone of a successful campaign. Basically, it contains the information you want people to know at the time, compiled in a clear and readable form. As it can be the first thing anyone reads about your campaign, they may make snap judgements about your group based on its content and presentation.

A leaflet is an extremely useful tool, as it can be given to anyone and everyone who is looking for information on the campaign – from school children doing projects, to potential donors, volunteers and patrons. A leaflet can launch the campaign, informing people of its aims, main arguments and who is running it. It can update people on campaign developments and progress, how the politicians are responding and the level of support. It will also show people what they can do to help.

You may decide to produce one at the beginning, followed by more as the campaign develops.

Distribution

Leaflets can be widely distributed. You could organise a door-to-door drop, with volunteers taking responsibility to cover certain streets or roads. Send a copy to all the relevant organisations, organise a press conference to announce its main message, send it to all your politicians, hand it out when you are gathering petitions, at public meetings, or information stalls. You may get permission to place bundles of them in local Community/Health Centres, shops, hairdressers', sports' clubs, restaurants, bars, libraries and dentists' and doctors' surgeries. You may be in a position to provide cardboard dispensers or stands for them which can be placed on counters, for all to see.

Warning! – The leaflet will probably take double the amount of time you expect to produce. Set deadlines, try to stick to them, but leave a little time over, just in case. In other words don't prepare a media launch of the leaflet until you are pretty sure it is ready. The delays can occur at all stages – writing, vetting, lay-out and printing.

Fliers and Newsletters

Fliers are usually brief and inform people of a particular event. They can be just a single sheet, and quite small (A4 is easy to photocopy and makes a good poster). They are useful for letting people know about a fund-raising event or encouraging them to attend your next public meeting. Just as with a leaflet, you will want to send out the right message, in a clear and eye-catching form, so many of the steps outlined in 'How to produce a good leaflet' will be relevant. Distribution will focus around the people you want to come to the event.

Newsletters are usually produced to keep people regularly informed on campaign developments. You may decide to produce them internally for your group members, supporters and patrons, or you may distribute them more widely – to your politicians, to the residents in your catchment area and through local organisations. It's a good idea to set up a sub-group with direct responsibility for deciding on content and overseeing general production. You might ask for articles and other material from your group members, or from relevant sources outside. If you are promising to produce your newsletter at certain times, stick to that, as people will come to expect their regular update. If it doesn't appear on time, they are likely to jump to conclusions, either about your organisational abilities, or about the progress of the campaign.

Internet

The Internet is a worldwide computer network, with information stored all over the globe, and accessible from your own home. (For details about the Internet, see Chapter 4: Access to Information.)

What if you wanted to get your campaign message and details of what is going on into this system, and accessible to millions of people around the world? Would it be useful to you to be able to publish a colour brochure on computer, update it as you please and have it available to 'Net users the world over?

If you think that the answer might be 'Yes', then consider setting up your own website. A website is just like an address on the 'Net, at which you can store information, images and even sound. You can design a website quite easily yourself, or get someone to do it for you. Next you will need an Internet Service Provider, or ISP, to allow you put this website on their computer, thereby making it accessible to all 'Net users. The charge for this will vary, depending on the amount of information that you wish to publish, and the amount of space it takes up on the ISP's hardware.

Campaign groups around the world are making use of the Internet to promote their causes. It might help your campaign – if you think so, then give it some thought, and get some advice.

Public Meetings

Public meetings are a great opportunity for getting your message across to a large and diverse group of people, and to gauge the amount of support out there. Question time at the end gives you a chance to find out what people want to know and to develop your arguments in more detail.

To have the maximum effect they need to be publicised and well-organised. Make sure that you have a worthwhile attendance, as a poor turnout could reflect badly on the campaign.

After each meeting, it's well worth assessing how it went. From this you can work out ways in which you could improve participation.

Petitions

While petitions are primarily a lobbying tool, the promotional element of collecting signatures cannot be ignored.

Gathering signatures helps to give your campaign a profile on the ground. It gives you a reason for going to where people are, rather than waiting for them to come to you. Your volunteers can talk to people, fill them in on the details of the campaign, inform them of the facts, answer questions, distribute leaflets, and recruit willing volunteers, all while standing there waving a clip-board! (For further details and 'HOW TO' see Chapter 9: Political Lobbying.)

Information Stalls

There are various benefits in setting up an information stall in a strategic and busy location. As well as getting the basic message across, you'll be in a position to raise money, increase the profile of the group and campaign, recruit new volunteers and gather new information.

There can be very little involved in setting up an information stand. Your stall doesn't have to be purpose built, a simple and handy fold-away wallpaper table with a banner as a backdrop is quite sufficient. As well as your campaign information – leaflets, newsletters, fliers, posters and so on – have a collection box on the table, a pile of membership and volunteer forms and any campaign merchandise you have for sale.

Wherever you plan to put your stand, *check with someone in authority* that it's okay to set up there. This might be the management of a shopping centre, the Gardaí or your Local Authority. A spot in a public area is usually free of charge, but you may have to pay for space at organised events – unless the organisers are sympathetic.

Notice Boards

They can be used for regular progress updates, news on upcoming meetings, events or fund-raisers as well as passing on the basic campaign information.

Use existing notice boards in libraries, schools, churches, community centres, workplaces, cafes, supermarkets and shopping centres – with the permission of the management in each place, of course.

Otherwise, you could create your own! Having a campaign notice board in some prominent place in the community could be an effective way of keeping people up-to-date. Anyone who is interested would then know where to check up on what's happening in the campaign.

Talks and Workshops

Talks and workshops are a good way of informing people about your work. You could set up a programme of events over a number of weeks which would both educate and update current and new members. Your local library or community centre may be available to you for this.

Window Displays

A shop or business in your area may be sympathetic enough to allow you to mount an exhibition in their window, or even just display a few posters. This would catch the passing interest of existing supporters, as well as those who may not be so familiar with your work.

Campaign related materials, such as information leaflets, posters, newspaper articles, photographs and merchandise are suitable and should be used to create an eye-catching window display.

HOW TO COMPILE A LIST OF PATRONS

Brainstorm amongst yourselves who you think might be useful and willing, and with whom you feel your campaign should be associated.

Your list might include:-

- Well known people and celebrities living in the campaign's catchment area

- Well known people who have supported similar campaigns in the past

- A cross section of patrons, appealing to a cross-section of the population from the world of music, art, film, sport, business, academia, law and the media

Be careful about including politicians, as you may not want to be seen to be favouring one party or politician over another.

From this, compile a list of people to approach.

Find out their contact addresses (and telephone numbers, if freely available).

Ask around amongst the group, your friends and people 'in the know', to see if you have a link through to any of the suggested people. They will be more likely to agree and to have faith in the campaign if the idea is proposed by someone they know. A direct contact also saves time.

Send a letter of request, clearly explaining who the group is and what you are trying to do. Be sure to enclose a copy of your leaflet and any other informational material and let them know that you are available to discuss the campaign in more detail if they wish.

Be sure to send a thank-you letter to all those who respond positively.

As people are often extremely busy, your letter can get lost in a pile of post, so it's worth sending a reminder if you have not heard anything after two weeks or so.

You could follow up request letters with a phone call. However, while this will show that you are keen and determined, some people may feel that they are being hassled, or that you have invaded their privacy, particularly if you have got hold of their home phone number through dubious means!

Keep your patrons well informed on campaign developments by sending regular updates, copies of new leaflets and your newsletters. Invite them to events and social gatherings.

HOW TO PRODUCE A GOOD LEAFLET

Give one person the job of compiling the leaflet, work out who will make suggestions on content, and who will vet the finished product.

Work out what the broad content of the leaflet will be, breaking it up under headings, and then check and comment on the drafts as they are produced.

The writer should avail of any assistance necessary, for instance, roping in someone with editing experience to help with the wording, or someone to do the lay-out.

When you are happy with the wording and lay-out, it should be circulated for final vetting. This could be done at a meeting, or better still, sent to people beforehand, so that they can have a good look at it and maybe voice their opinions individually to the writer.

Tips

Try to avoid a situation where too many people are advising on the content of the leaflet. You could end up going round in circles, haggling over words and getting nothing written.

Unless you are very lucky, the final version will be a compromise for some , but you can't please all of the people all of the time!

Try to find a friendly printer, who will do the job for free or cheaply.

Good lay-out and spacing is crucial. Without it your leaflet will be too wordy and seem difficult to read. Check for spelling and grammatical errors.

Include diagrams and photographs to bring the text alive.

Make sure to check your facts so that you will not be accused of spreading misinformation.

Put a catchy slogan on the cover, with a picture depicting your message to catch people's attention and encourage them to read further.

Always include a 'What You Can Do' section, outlining practical tasks anyone can do. For instance, writing to the relevant politicians (include the list of names and where they can be contacted), becoming a campaign volunteer, sending a donation or writing to the newspapers. Include a coupon, which they can fill in and send back – giving their names and addresses and ticking whether they want to become volunteers or supporters, and whether they are enclosing a donation.

You may want to include a letter which people can cut out, sign and send to the relevant person in power. For those who want to write in their own words, it will give an idea of what to ask for.

HOW TO ORGANISE PUBLIC MEETINGS

Venue

Location – Pick a well known Church/Community Hall/Hotel if your campaign is locally based. For a large campaign maybe the Town or City Hall. Or you may want to hold it outside, at the end of a march, for instance.

Accessibility – Pick a place that is easy to find and to get to. If people don't have cars, make sure it is within walking distance or else is well served by public transport. If they are travelling by car, can they park nearby? Try to ensure that the venue is accessible to old folk and people with disabilities. If steps are unavoidable, make sure that someone is around to offer help.

Space – Always pick a space that suits the number of people you expect to attend. There's nothing more de-moralising than a meeting where the hall is practically empty. Alternatively,while a packed room is great, you don't want to lose a bunch of supporters who can't get in.

Cost – As with everything, try to avoid spending too much money. Many halls or rooms are available at a very low cost, sometimes you can wangle to get one rent free, especially if people avail of any bar facilities afterwards. Be careful not to decide on a venue purely because it is free.

Heating – Always make sure that the space is warm, but not too hot and stuffy, and well ventilated, so that people can be comfortable.

Sound – Most halls or large spaces require amplification, so that everyone can hear what is being said. Hotels may have in-house systems, but be sure to check the price, as it will not necessarily be included in the hire fee. If you have to bring in your own equipment, you'll probably be able to get it from a local sound hire company, but don't forget to book in advance. Be sure that they help you set it up, or else that you have someone who knows how to do it on the night. It's a good idea to get a roving mike, so that people who speak from the floor can also be clearly heard.

Speakers' platform – Be sure that the speakers will be seen by the audience, or crowd. If a stage or podium is not available, then bring along your own sectioned platform (may be available from a local school or church hall), or improvise, taking safety into consideration of course!

Insurance – Be careful not to assume that insurance is only the venue owner's responsibility. They will be insured for anything that happens as a direct result of their negligence, such as a chair collapsing. But if someone trips up whilst walking to their seat, the organising body could indeed be liable. So it's best to get some advice early on. If your group is likely to hold a lot of public events and meetings, both indoors and outside, you may decide to take out long-term cover.

Safety – Be sure that the venue has enough fire escapes, that they are not locked, and that fire extinguishers have been recently checked. At the outset of the meeting you should make people aware of their whereabouts.

Check whether there's a first aid box on the premises. In any case, always bring your own, and try to make sure that someone in your group knows what to do if an accident happens. If your group plans to be around for a while, there's no harm in sending a few people on a First Aid course ... just in case!

Timing

Obviously when you hold the event it will have to fit in with your campaign strategy and the availability of the venue, but it is important also to pick a time that will suit your proposed audience. Should it be during the day or at night? If outside, do you want to catch passing shoppers? Would 1.00pm be good so as to get people on their lunch-breaks? A weekend or weekday night? 7.30pm or 8.30pm? Be careful not to clash with other popular events such as an Irish soccer match!

Set a start and end time.

Format

Aims – Be clear on the purpose of the meeting, what you want to achieve, and whom it is aimed at. Do you want to inform a new group of people about your campaign? To jizz them into action? To update them on developments? To get them to donate funds? To recruit volunteers? To encourage and inform existing supporters? For a show of strength?

Speakers – How many speakers do you want? Who will these be? Do you want to invite anyone from outside, to have people relating personal stories? Work out with them what they will say – so that all angles are covered and no one gets too boring.

Agenda – Decide who will chair the meeting and agree on the appropriate order of speakers, giving each a certain amount of time, and leaving a space at the end for questions from the floor. Be sure to let all speakers know how much time they have, so as to prevent speeches that are either too long or too short.

Politicians – Decide on whether you want to invite local and/or national politicians. If you feel they should be there, do you want to allot them a time to speak from the panel or from the floor, or will you leave it up to them to say their piece during question-time?

Media – Is this a meeting that you want reported in the press? Do you feel confident that it will reflect well on your group, and not degenerate into a free-for all slagging match? If so, invite them along, and ensure that your Press Officer looks after them.

The Opposition – Do you want to invite them to speak, to give their side of the argument, or answer questions from the floor? If so, be careful that the event doesn't get hi-jacked and turned into a PR stunt for them. Alternatively, you may feel that your meeting is for getting your points across, and that they should organise their own way. In that case, because the meetings will be open to the public, you cannot prevent the 'Opposition' from turning up, but your Chairperson can make it clear that you don't welcome their participation.

Pre-Publicity

As with all other public events, be sure to inform people in good time, but not too far in advance so that they forget. You can put up posters on lamp posts, in shop windows, on community notice boards. Organise door-to-door leaflet drops. Contact all the relevant media notice boards. (See under Promotion in Chapter 7: Media.) Tell all your existing supporters to come along. As with the publicity for fund-raising and public protests, this provides another chance for people to see your group's name, and to be aware that your campaign is very alive and active.

On the Night/Day

- Arrange for a number of people to get to the venue early, to put out the chairs, set up the PA system, make sure the heating's on.

- Hang up any promotional material, posters, banners or whatever behind the speakers' platform. Put up your information stand at the back of the hall, complete with petition sheets, volunteer and/or membership forms, so that people can browse before or after the meeting. Be sure that members of your group are there to answer any questions and to encourage people to join.

- Get people to sign an attendance book as they arrive.

- You may want to pass petition sheets around during the meeting, so that people who have to rush off at the end have had a chance to sign up.

- Be sure to start on time, or at least not more than ten minutes late. Keep the meeting snappy, particularly if you are all standing around outside in the cold. Don't let question-time get out of hand!

- Give someone the job of running around with the roving mike during question-time, someone who is assertive enough to grab it back off a speaker who is rambling on .

If you are looking for donations, make sure that this is made clear – a quick run-down on the campaign's financial situation from your Treasurer during the meeting does no harm at all – put the donation hat or box in a prominent position, preferably get someone to hold it under people's noses as they go out the door!

COMPASSION IN WORLD FARMING
HETTY THE HEN

Compassion in World Farming *is an international organisation which campaigns on farm-animal welfare issues. The Irish branch is based in Cork.*

There are many very worthy causes, and many important events taking place on any given day. To get your particular cause noticed, you may have to do something eye-catching and of interest to the media. In addition, your message to the public needs to be simple, something which can be absorbed in as little time as possible, and unforgettable. One of the best ways of satisfying all these criteria is to use a visual image based on a 'prop'.

One of the most successful props used by Compassion in World Farming (CIWF) was **Hetty** the battery hen (who was in fact an eight foot tall costume worm by a volunteer). We took Hetty, and a human-sized battery cage, on a flying tour of Ireland in 1993.

The combination of Hetty looking on whilst people crammed into a battery cage proved wonderful for media photographs!. Featherless and pink, Hetty looked marvellous in colour. To add to the image, the CIWF team wore dark green CIWF sweatshirts emblazoned on the front with the simple and easily remembered message: 'Go Free Range'. Even for radio interviews, it was a great opening line to talk about Hetty the giant hen travelling around Ireland!

With regard to getting our message accross, the visual impression to the public was attention-grabbing, immediate and unforgettable. It needed only one step of the imagination for people to understand the very real plight of battery hens, aided by a huge photograph mounted on an A-frame, showing hens inside a battery shed.

The subject of battery hens is very sad and depressing; there is nothing amusing about it at all. But the fact is that Hetty worked by making the point and getting media coverage. She left a lasting impression in people's mind: three years on, I still meet people who remember the interview on Gay Byrne's radio show about Hetty! Hopefully, people will think of her when buying eggs, and will as a result choose to 'Go Free Range' .

Mary-Anne Bartlett, Director, Compassion in World Farming.

7
WORKING WITH THE MEDIA

'There's no such thing as bad publicity, except your obituary.'
Brendan Behan, Irish playwright.

INTRODUCTION

Good coverage in the media provides a way of communicating the group's message to a wider audience, which helps in getting supporters, donors and volunteers. For many people, good media presentation of an issue gives it credibility and a degree of importance.

When the media highlights an issue, it often brings it to centre stage. Newspapers and news programmes are followed enthusiastically by government press officers, and by national and local politicians.

We should remember that the relationship between journalists or reporters and campaign groups is mutually dependent. Just as we need them, they need us to provide good stories and up-to-date information.

This chapter aims to help you to do this in the most effective way possible, by taking you through the necessary structures, strategies and methods.

MEDIA STRATEGY

Just as a group must put a strategy in place around which its campaign can be constructed, it should approach the vital area of media work in the same way. Putting an effective structure in place to deal with media-related work will ensure that the group's activities and message will be covered in full.

Form a Media Sub-group

Charged with co-ordinating the group's presentation of the campaign to the media, the Media Sub-group should be made-up of a number of people who can speak on behalf of the group, and a Press Officer with overall responsibility. They should make sure that there is a spokesperson available to the media at all times.

They should be in constant touch with all elements of the campaign, and should have input into all planning at an early stage – making sure that the campaign is media-friendly from the beginning.

The Press Officer should attend the Co-ordinating Committee meetings, where overall policy in relation to the media is decided and media plans agreed.

Develop a Media Plan

This is a diary of events which should encourage media interest in the campaign. These might be external events which could be taken advantage of, as well as those organised by the group.

This plan should be drawn up hand-in-hand with the campaign Action Plan. (See Chapter 2: Structure.)

Gather a List of Suitable Interviewees

The Media Committee should continually be on the look-out for good people who are willing to talk about their personal reasons for supporting the campaign, residents affected by the problem, people with interesting stories to tell, celebrities and maybe some experts. Feature writers or radio show presenters will be very keen to talk to a wide selection of speakers.

Prepare a Media List

A good media list contains contact names, addresses, phone and fax numbers for all media contacts. This makes the job of sending out press information or ringing around much easier, and ensures that no-one is missed out.

This list should be updated regularly.

A comprehensive media list is available in the IPA Diary.

Build Good Relationships with Reporters and Journalists

Having a personal approach and getting to know your reporters and journalists usually helps the two-way relationship between you and them. Once you have developed a relationship be loyal to your contact. If you are open and honest with them, they will generally return the favour, and may push for coverage on your behalf.

MEDIA TOOLS

Well put together notices and documents, and properly arranged press conferences and photo opportunities greatly improve your chances of coverage.

Advance Notices

Press and Photo Opportunity Notices are for letting the media know in advance of any forthcoming event which you would like them to cover. They should be clear, short and simple, and should be printed on your own letter-headed paper. Include the name and contact number of your Press Officer for further information.

Press Notice

A Press Notice is used to inform the media of a forthcoming event and should include information on the five Ws :-

Who is organising the event?
What is happening?
Why is it being organised?
When will it take place?
Where will it take place?

Photo Opportunity Notice

A Photo Opportunity notice is very similar to a Press Notice, but will emphasise the visual impact of the event. It should be sent directly to the Photo Desk of a newspaper. This applies in cases where the Photo Opportunity is just a part of an event, such as a protest, as well as where it is an event in its own right.

While TV reporters are always accompanied by camera crews, national newspapers have Photo Editors who work independently alongside the newsdesks. As all photographers want to take the best picture, if it is obvious that you are making an effort to make sure that this is possible, they will be more likely to attend.

Press Release

A Press Release can be prepared to give details of a news item, to interest a journalist in doing a feature article on the organisation and its activities, to get a slot on a radio/TV show, or to summarise reports, publications, or important speeches. It generally includes quotes from your spokesperson, and some background information on the campaign. It is either distributed to journalists at an event you are holding, or issued directly to the media.

While many journalists will want to get some direct quotes from your spokesperson, some newspaper stories are taken word-for-word from the Press Release. This makes the content and wording quite important. You need to work out what you want people to know, and then to present the story in such a way that it is interesting and readable.

Photo Opportunity

The importance of providing good photographs for the media cannot be overestimated. Good pictures, or TV footage can often make the difference between a story being reported or not. An impressive photograph is likely to catch the attention of the reader and encourage them to follow the story. In many cases the visual image is what remains in the memory.

Be creative!

Press Conference

A Press Conference is a form of meeting at which a number of speakers address the media and answer questions. It is used when a simple Press Release or Photo Opportunity is not enough. You may want to launch a new campaign, announce the publication of a report or focus on new and important information. It is also a good way to respond to some outrage by the 'Rogue' or better still to celebrate a success.

Press Pack

A good Press Pack should be distributed at Press Conferences or any media events you organise. It is also handy to have a number of basic Packs on file ready to be given to journalists or other interested people who need background information on the campaign.

Present the contents neatly in A4 folders or envelopes.

The following could be included:-

- Press Release.

- Texts of statements to be made at the Conference.

- A summary, if a report is being launched.

- Background material on the campaign, such as leaflets and fact sheets.

- Supplementary material, giving more detailed information on the issue.

- Relevant photographs, 8' by 10' black & white glossies, if you can afford them.

- Examples of campaign PR material, such as car stickers, posters, post-cards.

MEDIA PRESENTATION

How you present the message is as important as the message itself. Time spent on practice and preparation should improve your chances of getting through to people.

Many people feel quite nervous about talking to the media. To help you gain confidence and experience, it is useful to organise a Media Training Course for all your potential spokespeople. In the meantime, the following are useful pointers.

Preparation

- Anytime you talk to a reporter always be prepared. It's best to work out media statements in advance. Role play interviews, on the phone and face-to-face, practising answers to the most obvious and difficult questions. Think of interesting stories relevant to the campaign which you can tell.

- If you know you are going to get just a sound-bite (a few sentences, say, for a news programme) prepare a short, clear statement in advance. Since the amount of air time is short you want to be sure to get your message across. If you make long statements and the item is pre-recorded you will be giving the news editor the control to decide which part of your message to deliver to the public, sometimes leading to comments being taken out of context.

- Never presume that the news journalist covering your story knows very much about your campaign, even if the newspaper or radio station has covered the issue in the past. Often news reporters are given the job at the last minute and will not have had any time to do background reading.

- Dress appropriately for TV – decide when it's best to wear a suit, jeans or your campaign T-shirt. You don't want to offend your potential audience, or perhaps marginalise the cause. Being untidy is off-putting, and will take from what you say. Dressing in accordance with personal beliefs may not always be appropriate.

Content

- When speaking to the media it's important to tell stories and personal experiences, to give practical examples which the ordinary reader, viewer or listener can relate to. Make the issue come alive. Try to speak personally, in such a way that people can identify with you.

- When answering questions, avoid listing a ream of facts and statistics. Few people are interested in or understand the minute details. You need to get your message across in such a way that you encourage people to feel as strongly as you do about the issue.

- If asked something you know little about, rather than making up an answer, say you don't know. Tell them that you will make an effort to find out for them, but be sure that you mean it.

- There is no obligation on anyone to answer questions. It is okay to tell a reporter that they have raised a subject that your group is not prepared to discuss at this time.

- Be careful with 'off-the-record' statements or information, especially if it is someone you don't know. It is different when you are dealing with a reporter with whom you have a good relationship – you should be able to give them information which you don't want used.

- Avoid catch phrases and jargon, especially abbreviations and technical terms.

- Always tell the truth.

Tone

- It can be good to appear vulnerable, as sympathy always goes to the underdog. However, don't whine – people hate whingers.

- While it's important not to hide your emotion, beware of sounding fanatical or too aggressive.

GETTING COVERAGE

Bringing together your Media Strategy and the tools available to you, it's time to get your message into the media for all to see.

News Coverage

News coverage generally focuses on current events as they happen or are unfolding, 'Old news is no news.' It's unlikely that your news will be covered if it reaches the media too late.

While features are often exclusive, news items will be covered by a wide spectrum of newspapers and TV/ radio newsdesks who try to present them in an objective and balanced manner.

The following guidelines will help to ensure widespread news coverage of a planned event, protest, press conference or launch:-

- Check that your media list is up-to-date. Work out whom you want to contact, widening the net as much as possible. Be aware that newspapers have different readerships. For example, the *Irish Times* is read by politicians and professionals, many of whom are based in Dublin. The *Irish Independent* has a wide circulation amoungst rural communities. The timing of the event will determine whether it is worth contacting the evening or Sunday papers.

- Fax, hand-deliver or post a Press Notice to the News Editors of the relevant newspapers, radio and TV stations, to arrive two/three days before the planned event (up to five days if you want a camera crew). Send one to any journalist with whom you may have a good relationship. It is a wise practice to keep them informed. Even if they are not on duty at the stated time, they may well put a word in on your behalf to ensure coverage.

- Send a Photo Opportunity Notice to all Photo Editors, where appropriate.

- Phone the relevant News/Photo desks to check that the Notices were received, and that the event is listed in their diary. You can ask whether it is likely that they will attend, but don't be put off if the answer is vague or abrupt. Often the decision about what stories are to be covered is made at the last minute, and depends on other events of the day. It is very important however to make this verbal contact, as too often Press Notices get lost, and the event is not recorded in the diary. If you get to talk to the journalists, you can convince them of the importance of the event and why they should be there.

- Prepare a Press Release, which is then given out to the journalists at the event itself, or faxed/hand-delivered afterwards to those who did not attend.

It is very useful to have a mobile phone with you on the day, so that radio stations in particular can make contact (or you can phone them) to do a quick 'on-the-spot' interview which would generally be carried on the hourly News.

Feature Coverage

Feature coverage is more varied than news in both content and format. It generally takes a more in-depth view of the issue – TV documentary, radio debate, illustrated articles or personal stories in magazines and feature or specialist pages of newspapers (often in the Weekend edition). The story itself might be one-sided, but balance might be achieved by further stories on the same page or programme, or within the series. Generally, features are planned a couple of weeks in advance of publication, or in the case of magazines even one to two months ahead.

Guidelines for getting feature coverage:-

- Decide which newspapers, magazines, radio or TV shows are appropriate to your campaign. Before approaching Radio/TV producers, work out which Shows you want to appear on, in order of preference, then approach them accordingly. In RTÉ in particular, there is a very clear hierarchy. The chat shows with wider audiences, both on radio and television, are highly competitive and so often want exclusives, or at least a unique angle to the story. They don't like taking items which have already been covered elsewhere in the station.

- Send a Press Pack or a Press Notice along with a letter explaining why your issue will be of interest to the public, and listing possible interviewees, to the Features Editor or radio/TV Show Producer or Researcher.

- Follow up with a phone call, or if possible, arrange a meeting to discuss the matter further.

- When looking for feature articles in the print media, it is a good idea to offer different angles and spokespeople to the different papers.

Local Media Coverage

Coverage in the local media, both on radio and in newspapers is crucial to all local campaigns. It is also very important to the development of national campaigns, a fact which is often overlooked, particularly if the group has its base in Dublin.

Guidelines for local media coverage:-

- If the campaign is local, work out which radio stations and newspapers are appropriate to your catchment area. In the case of a national campaign, first decide which areas you want to target, and then list the corresponding media. The IPA Diary has a full list of all the regional media in the country. (See Chapter 4: Access to Information.)

- The procedure for getting local coverage is similar to that for news and features. You will fare better if, at an early stage, you have built up a good working relationship with someone in the station or newspaper office. Arrange a meeting with the editor, producer or station manager, at which you give them a full Press Pack and convince them of the importance of your cause.

- Keep in regular phone contact with them, giving updates on your activities, and making sure that they are invited to all press events well in advance. Most local media organisations do not have very many staff, so they are not always able to send people out at short notice.

Reacting to Adverse Coverage

If you feel upset by a newspaper's account of your story or a presenter's attitude in an interview, don't scream down the phone. Take time to assess the impact of the report on others. It may not be half as bad as you feared. If you really need to raise the issue with the journalist involved, wait until you have calmed down and then discuss it carefully. File the knowledge of how they behave for future reference. If you want to call for a correction, bear in mind that few people will read it, and decide whether it's worth getting into a row to maybe achieve very little. It's usually better to respond through the Letters to the Editor page.

If you feel certain important newspapers, or TV/radio presenters are unsupportive or are even hostile, look for creative and positive ways of convincing them of the value of your campaign.

If this fails, don't waste time in battle. Focus on getting good coverage through other means.

Other Routes into the Media

While a group will normally concentrate on getting news and maybe features coverage, it should not neglect other opportunities in the media. Only by having an overall media strategy and considering all routes can you hope to get the most coverage.

Letters to the editor

In general, Editors use this section of the newspaper to keep readers up-to-date on issues which they do not necessarily comment on themselves, and to give people a chance to argue with each other.

It is a useful campaign tactic to sustain an on-going debate on your issue through the Letters Page. While obviously letters can be written on behalf of your organisation, it is important to encourage as many of your supporters as possible to write in on their own behalf. This can be done over a period of time, or there may be occasions when it is appropriate to 'blitz' the Page, for example in response to a recent letter from the 'opposition'. Be sure that your Press Officer keeps an eye on the relevant Letters Pages, and if needs be organises a phone-around to set the pens in motion.

A few points to keep in mind

- Keep the letters brief, clear and to-the-point.

- Try to be original.

- Type if possible, and be sure to include your full name, address and telephone number. The inclusion of your phone number is necessary so that the Editor's staff can check the authenticity of the letter. Your number will not be printed, but your address will, unless you request otherwise.

- Fax, E-mail or send the letter directly to the Letters Page, and phone to ensure that it has been received.

- Don't be disappointed if your letter isn't printed immediately. It may take a few days to appear.

Opinion pieces

Some papers accept one-off pieces from people about their own views and experiences. It is different from other forms of coverage in that you get to write the piece yourself, but it will appear as just another article in the paper. There are obvious restrictions as to what you can write – the paper would not print anything which it deemed libellous for instance.

Approach newspapers in the same way as you would for features coverage.

Phone-ins

There are a number of programmes on local and national radio, which offer listeners the chance to ring in. You may be able to get the story of your campaign onto such programmes as a story in itself, particularly when there has been an important development. You could also phone in with comments on related stories, or ask questions of a guest on the programme who is relevant to your campaign, such as a local politician or developer.

Media Notice Boards

Most local radio stations and local and national newspapers have diary listings or community notice board slots, which will advertise details of events free of charge. This is a good way of informing the public about your protest rallies, public meetings or fund-raisers.

You will need to do a bit of research to find out which papers or radio stations give this service, on what days, and how far in advance you have to send in the information. Add the details to your Media List.

Advertisements

The only way to communicate exactly what you want to say through the media is to pay for it! Where you have a high level of public support, local media might be willing to give you a reduced rate.

Advertising, for campaign groups, usually consists of the campaign message accompanied by an appeal for support and funds. Newspaper ads are the normal route for this, and should include a support coupon. If your group feels that they need to advertise, then look at all of the many options available.

KEEPING RECORDS

It is a good idea to record all press cuttings featuring, or relevant to, your campaign in a large ring folder or file. In case you may need to make photocopies, cut each one out carefully and stick onto an A4 sheet, making sure to mark the date and name of the publication clearly.

Likewise, be sure to video-tape all TV appearances and record radio items. It's useful to look at these afterwards and if necessary to discuss how presentation can be improved in the future.

HOW TO PREPARE A PRESS RELEASE

Many people feel intimidated by the thought of writing Press Releases, but they are really not that difficult to prepare once you follow a number of basic steps.

Lay-out is important as it makes your story more readable and may save editorial time – remember that occasionally the text itself may be used directly as copy.

- The content of the Press Release should be typed, double-spaced on one side of A4 headed paper, with wide margins of about 50mm on either side. This margin can be used by the editor for comments.

- The organisation's name and address should be clearly marked.

- Type date on left hand corner, with 'FOR IMMEDIATE RELEASE' clearly stated, if the Release concerns something that has already happened. If you do not want it released before a certain time, instead, in the corner, put 'EMBARGO – NOT TO BE USED BEFORE.......', naming a time and date before which the Release cannot be used.

- Do not type main text in capitals.

- Don't underline the text for emphasis. Underlining is an editor's instruction to the typesetter.

- If the release runs to more than one page 'contd' or 'more' should be marked at the bottom right hand corner, with the following page(s) numbered in the top left hand corner.

- Sentences should not run from one page to the next.

- At the bottom of the release write 'Ends'.

- Clearly mark the name and phone number of your Press Officer for further information.

- Try to think up a catchy heading to the story which will attract the journalist's attention. Type in capitals above the first paragraph.

It's important to keep the release as short and simple as possible. Make sure that the first paragraph has the bones of the story to catch the journalists' attention, and encourage them to read further. Be sure to state the facts as clearly as possible. Beware of jargon.

Try to be forceful, not aggressive, enthusiastic without being too emotional.

The use of direct quotes from your spokesperson adds life and a personal slant to the story. It will also give an idea of what your spokesperson is likely to say if the journalist decides to do a more in-depth interview.

EXAMPLES: EAST TIMOR CAMPAIGN PRESS RELEASES

The **East Timor Campaign** *is a grass roots country-wide campaign, which aims to raise awareness of the on-going human rights situation and the illegal occupation of East Timor by Indonesia. It disseminates information at numerous levels – political, media and community.* Tom Hyland, Co-ordinator

E.T.I.S.C.

East Timor Ireland Solidarity Campaign
210, Le Fanu Road, Ballyfermot, Dublin 10. Ireland. Tel. / Fax: 6233148

PRESS RELEASE   PRESS RELEASE   PRESS RELEASE

XANANA'S TRIAL, INDONESIA'S SHAME
Dublin 15 May 1993

Attention News Editor.

The trial of the Timorese resistance leader Xanana Gusmao has been a farce and requires immediate international scrutiny and denunciation.
Since his capture in November 1992 he was visited only once by the delegates of the International Committee of the Red Cross (ICRC).
The reputation of his military appointed lawyer, Mr Sudjono, is very low among colleagues and has given rise to cynicism and serious concern.
Attempts by Xanana's immediate relatives in East Timor and Australia to engage the services of well-known human rights lawyers from the prestigious Jakarta-based Legal Aid Institute (LBH) were opposed by the military who preferred the more pliable, inexperienced and obscure Mr Sudjono.
The president of the ICRC, Mr Sommaruga, stated last week in Jakarta that ICRC access to East Timor and prisoners in the occupied territory has not been satisfactory. Indonesia's deliberate actions to undermine the mandate of the Geneva-based humanitarian organisation has been in violation of it's obligations under international humanitarian law.
Mr. Jose Ramos Horta, exiled Foreign Minister of East Timor said to-day;
"The Indonesian authorities have no jurisdiction over East Timor under international law. Indonesian leaders responsible for the conduct of the war in East Timor are guilty of war crimes and crimes against humanity".
Referring to the legal charade levelled against Xanana Gusmao, Mr. Horta said;
"The Indonesian military authorities are a law unto themselves and have not had even the pretence of according the defendant the appearance of a fair hearing. They have refused him the right to speak Portuguese which is his first language".
Commenting on the trial, Tom Hyland of E.T.I.S.C. says "Xanana Gusmao is to the East Timorese what Nelson Mandela is to the people of South Africa".

For more information contact Shirley Moran or Brendan Mc Keon at 6233148 day or evening.

Patrons:
Mike Allen
Robert Ballagh
Mary Banotti M.E.P.
Monica Barnes T.D.
Prof. Terence Browne
Fr. Dennis Carroll
Dr. Eamonn Casey
Pat Cox M.E.P.
Martin Collins
Prionsias De Rossa T.D.
Bobby Egar
Des Geraghty M.E.P.
Michael D. Higgins T.D.
Sr. Stanislaus Kennedy
Brendan Kennelly
Peadar Kirby
Soizick Le Saux
Nell McCafferty
Mary McEvoy
Gerry McCarthy
Mwende Munuve
Don Mullan
Joe Murray
Senator David Norris
Fr. Sean O'Cuiv
Adi Roche
Dick Roche T.D.
Catriona Ruane
Senator Brendan Ryan
Pat Walsh

Director:
Tom Hyland

Secretary:
Kaye Ryan

Vol. Workers:
Martina Cranny
Jim Hurley
Brendan McKeon

BEFORE AND AFTER

*Compare the Press Release below with the one on the previous page
to get a sense of how attention to layout and the 'less is more'
approach can work in your favour.*

EAST TIMOR
Ireland Solidarity Campaign

Suite 13, 3rd Floor, Dame House
24-26 Dame Street, Dublin 2.
Tel/Fax 01 6719207
E-Mail etisc@indigo.ie

Honorary President
Xanana Gusmao

Nobel Patrons

Mairead Maguire
Archbishop Desmond Tutu

Patrons
Mike Allen
Brian Anderson
Niall Andrews MEP
Robert Ballagh
Mary Banotti MEP
Monica Barnes
Prof. Terence Browne
Denis Carroll
Dr. Eamonn Casey
Pat Cox MEP
Martin Collins
Sen. John Dardis
Prionsias De Rossa TD
Bobby Egar
Des Geraghty
Michael D Higgins TD
Hot Press
St. Stanislaus Kennedy
Prof. Brendan Kennealy
Peadar Kirby
Tom Kitt TD
Souzick Le Saux
Bernie Malone MEP
Nell Mc Cafferty
Eleanor McEvoy
Mary McEvoy
Paul McGrath
Patricia McKenna MEP
Don Mullan
Joe Murray
Sen. David Norris
Fr. Sean O'Cuiv
William Penrose TD
Adi Roche
Sen. Dick Roche
Catriona Ruane
Eoin Ryan TD
Brendan Ryan
Trevor Sargent TD
Pat Walsh

CHRISTMAS VIGIL AT DUTCH EMBASSY

PRESS RELEASE   23RD DECEMBER 1996

The annual East Timor Campaign Christmas vigil will take
place outside the Dutch embassy, Merrion Road,
Ballsbridge on Christmas day between 12.00 Noon
and 1. PM.   Since the East Timor Campaign was launched
five years ago, members and supporters have held an annual
Christmas Day vigil outside the diplomatic representation of
an EU country that supplies weapons to Indonesia. Also
taking part in the vigil will be members of the East Timorese
community now living in Ireland.

*" I think that it is important that we not lose sight of the
meaning of Christmas, which is one of peace and justice ",
said Tom Hyland of the East Timor Campaign.
Hyland went on to say, " Christmas is a time of reflection
and while this year there have been a number of
encouraging events with regard to East Timor, most
notably the awarding the awarding of the Nobel Peace
Prize to the East Timorese, we must also remember that
they continue to suffer on a daily basis".*

The Dutch government continue to supply military hardware
to the Suharto regime in Indonesia. It is also expected that
little effort will be put into ending the Indonesian occupation
of East Timor during the Dutch presidency because of
Dutch investments in Indonesia.

FOR MORE INFORMATION   671 9207 (DAY)
                                                      623 3148 (EVENING)

http://www.telematix.ie/East Timor/ETIndex.html

HOW TO ORGANISE A PHOTO OPPORTUNITY

Deciding What to Do

- If you are organising a public event, and are not sure if numbers will be significant, then focus on creating an image – dress a number of people in a costume which reflects your message or wear T-shirts printed with your slogan, display colourful banners and placards and locate the event at a visually relevant place.

- You may feel it is more appropriate to organise a visual 'stunt' which clearly shows your message yet requires fewer people. This falls under the heading of Street Theatre. (See Chapter 8: Public Protests.)

- You may want to give photographers a range of photo options. This would be particularly relevant for a features article, where the photographs might include campaigners handing out leaflets or collecting signatures on a petition.

- Photographers are often attracted by the fact that celebrities and well-known figures are supporting a campaign, so if any are attending your event be sure to let the media know.

- Don't overdo it. A Photo Opportunity that is too contrived could put off the press and the wider audience. Make sure that you are out to get across the campaign message, and not just looking for coverage for its own sake.

On the Day

- Bring your own photographer. While the larger papers prefer to use their own photographers, local and specialist press are more willing to use shots which may be printed elsewhere. In addition to supplying photographs to the press you will have good visual records for your own files and for future use in newsletters and leaflets. If sending in a photograph to a newspaper, include the name of the photographer for credibility purposes. Usually they like to receive 8' by 10' glossies rather than a matte finish.

- If you are organising a protest where there is the possibility of arrest or rough treatment, it's advisable to bring along your own stills photographer and video cameraman to film the events. If you are not notifying the media in advance, for fear of a leak interfering with your plans, this will ensure that you catch any useful footage. A professional photographer can wire this to the relevant newsdesks for immediate use.

- Be patient! Sometimes, photographers can appear impatient, or over-particular. You may find yourselves posing for ages while numerous shots are taken. Hang in there, it'll be worth it in the end.

- If you want the picture taken a certain way, talk to the photographer and explain what you feel is appropriate.

HOW TO ORGANISE A PRESS CONFERENCE

Be clear on why you are holding the Conference and what you want to say.

- Pick your speakers. It's usually best to have at least two. You may want to invite people with direct experience of the issue in question, an expert from outside the group, or a celebrity who supports your cause.

- Pick a chairperson. Their job is to direct the meeting and make sure that everything runs smoothly. This includes introducing the speakers and fielding questions from journalists.

- Set out an agenda. Make sure that everyone knows what they have to say, maybe role-playing beforehand.

- Arrange a suitable venue. In most cases the venue is determined by the nature of the conference: if you are launching a campaign, do it from your office-base; if you want to deliver a message to the Government, position yourselves near Dáil Éireann; or if you are complaining about a factory, hold it near the site. You may want to hold it outside, but be wary of rain, traffic and loud noise. It is often safer to use a hotel room or pub-space nearby, the costs of which may be reduced by a supportive manager or owner. When choosing your venue, bear in mind that it must be easily accessible to the media, some of whom may have to rush back to the office for deadlines, or onto another job. If you are hoping for national television or radio coverage try to hold the event in a town which has studio facilities.

- Arrange a suitable time. This may be determined by the content of your message, or by what other news items are listed for that day.

- Be sure to check to see that you are not clashing with any other big events – when in doubt ask a friendly journalist to scan the news diary. Set a time which suits any key journalists you wish to attend. If possible try to schedule the event for mid-morning around 10.30/11.00am – that way you will still catch the evening papers, whose deadline is midday, and also be in good time for the 6 o'clock News and the next day's dailies. Mondays and Tuesdays are usually quiet media days and so you can be more certain of a good attendance and more widespread coverage. Alternatively, more people read newspapers on Fridays and Saturdays, so your message, if printed, will have a wider audience. With more readers but less chance of coverage, it's a bit of a gamble, really.

- Fax Press and Photo Opportunity Notices to all the media two/three days in advance of the date. Phone around to make sure they have been received and to gauge the level of media interest.

- On the day, arrive early to ensure that all preparations are complete so that the conference will start on time. If using a hotel room, you may find that staff have already set it out in conventional conference style with a top table facing rows of chairs. If you are not expecting many people, or you feel the lay-out is too intimidating, it's best to re-arrange the furniture more informally – push the table aside and put a semi-circle of chairs around the speakers.

- Place banners or placards identifying your group in key positions so that any photos or TV footage of the speakers will also include the group name. This helps to promote your image at the same time as your message. Place any relevant literature or background information on a nearby table.

- Be sure that someone is near the door to welcome the journalists, to give each a Press Pack and to usher in late-comers.

- Keep speeches short and to the point, with plenty of time for questions. The Press Conference should not last more than about thirty to forty minutes if you want to keep people's interest.

- Provide tea, coffee and biscuits, and time for an informal chat afterwards.

- Despite all the best planning, your issue may still be scooped by a sex scandal or Government collapse – it's best to remain resolute and cheerful.

- Get your Press Release and Press Pack to all the media who didn't attend as soon as possible, and follow up with a phone call to see if they wish to hear more over the phone. Alternatively try to arrange an interview for a future date.

8
PUBLIC PROTESTS

'Passion and vision are essential, but without action they are empty.'
Dave Foreman, Environmental Activist
and founder of Earth First!

'Non-violence is the first article of my faith. It is also the last article of my creed.'

Mahatma Gandhi, Indian Statesman.

INTRODUCTION

The reality is that many of the problems we face in the world today cannot be solved by negotiation alone, and often we need to supplement our discussions, objections, and promotions, with a different approach. In running many types of campaign, there will come a point at which some form of public protest is useful, or even downright essential.

This chapter will take you through some of the circumstances which might make it necessary, provide you with some options on what form your protest should take and give you some guidelines on how to go about organising such activities.

FACTORS IN DECIDING ON SUITABLE FORMS OF PROTESTS

Protests can be a powerful campaign tool, and with the diversity of options available careful consideration is needed to choose the most effective one for your group at any given time.

The following factors should help you to decide:-

Stage of the campaign

Within the campaign, your choice might be affected by:-

Urgency – when time is on your side you can consider a wide range of options, and choose one which fits in neatly with your overall campaign strategy. Equally, if other approaches have failed and time is running short, it may be necessary to take fairly drastic action.

Opportunities arising – often an opening for some form of protest will present itself. An effective group must be able to recognise such chances and react, maybe very quickly, in order to make the best of them. In fact, you should be actively searching for such an opening.

Campaign fatigue – a time comes in many (or even most) campaigns when interest within the group is beginning to flag, when there seems to have been a lack of progress for a while, or when the public appears to have forgotten about your issue. This might be a good time to pull together some form of public protest, giving the group something concrete to focus on and boosting the campaign message.

An important consideration here is that a 'bad' protest, such as a poorly attended march, could have a demoralising effect, so you need to put in the effort to prevent that happening, and instead come up with an activity which will leave people feeling like they have made a difference.

What is Acceptable to the Group

The form of public protest chosen must sit well with the people in the group, and care should be taken to accommodate the differing views of those involved. A pitfall here, as with other attempts to operate by consensus, is that this leads to the lowest common denominator, and the mildest form of protest is opted for over a hard action. It would be more beneficial overall to thrash things out and to find a form which is acceptable to most people, without being too close to either of the extremes suggested.

The range of protests a group might opt for will probably change as members change, and also change over time. A conservative group might become more radical as it gets in new blood, and a radical group might 'mellow' as it ages.

What is Acceptable to the Section of the Community Involved or Targeted

Rarely can a campaign be fought in a vacuum, and the views of the public are very important. In the long term, it is the education of the public which will lay the groundwork for solving many issues. While this can often be too slow to meet immediate campaign aims, it must still be recognised as an essential element of campaign work.

How the public will respond to your protest is something you will need to give some thought to. You should aim to protest in such a way that the public understands the issue better, and respects you for the action you have taken. It is normally best not to upset people already on your side, or potential supporters.

An alternative approach is to shock people, if the situation demands that the public be awoken to some important issue. Bringing some condemnation on the group need not always be seen as a bad thing (since you are not going to please all of the people, all of the time) and could heighten the profile of the group more efficiently than other methods.

The important point here is that you consider how you want people to respond, and try to select a form of public protest which will come closest to achieving the desired response.

FORMS OF PUBLIC PROTESTS

Now that you have the considerations in mind, here's a broad breakdown of the options available. Within each category there is room for endless variation, so get your group thinking.

Marches and Demonstrations

At its simplest, the idea is to get people, preferably in large numbers, out onto the streets to highlight the campaign message. This means getting more than just those directly involved in the campaign motivated to protest, and so takes a certain amount of organising and publicising. It is a common and accepted way of airing grievances publicly in many parts of the world.

Some of the variations in this area include:-

- **March** – a protest on the hoof, generally with specified start and end points and laden with banners and placards.

- **Rally** – a mass protest at a particular location, usually a central public area, or at a site central to the campaign objective. As well as a stand-alone event, a rally is a good way to end a march, with the crowd being addressed by speakers.

  Both marches and rallies tend to be judged by the numbers attending, as this is taken as a measure of support for the campaign. Organisers should take particular note of this. Another influential factor is the tone of the protest, and this can be set by add-ins, such as music-drumming to show discontent, or lively tunes for celebration.

- **Vigil** – a solemn occasion might best be marked by a quiet protest at some appropriate spot. This is often done at night, and accompanied by candles.

- **Banner protest** – a few people standing with a banner and placards can be a worthwhile form of protest. Targeting a business or industrial premises, an event attended by a national figure, a public gathering, and so on, offers a small group of people the opportunity to get their message across.

In deciding which of these is most suitable, consider the number of people you can expect to attend and tailor the demonstration to that size.

Street Theatre

Street Theatre is a way of communicating directly with the public, using other media in addition to the spoken and written word. It consists of building a scene or image, using song, dance, mime, mimicry or just down-right taking the mickey!

Don't be put off by the title – this can range from a full festival of parody, down to a single person in costume with a placard. The aim is to create an image (or a series of images) which illustrates your message. The possibilities are endless, and include the use of masks, puppets, props and scenery, special constructions and 'St Patrick's Day'-style floats.

A single scene is possibly the easiest to create, and with some thought it offers a mode of protest which can be highly effective, forceful, memorable, and fun! An additional benefit is that the media are provided with an image, which improves your chances of coverage. This should be treated as a Photo Opportunity. (See Chapter 7: Role of the Media.)

To set you thinking, here are some examples:-

- A bed, parked in the centre of town, with two people in it wearing caricature masks to represent a local business man and a politician, could suggest collusion ('in bed with'). It would look well on the front of the paper.

- A lone figure, dressed as the Grim Reaper, could be used to draw peoples attention to some threat or danger which your group is trying to highlight.

- Surrounding an embassy with flowers and music could be a way of showing solidarity with the people of that country, while condemning the actions of their government.

Direct Action

This goes a number of steps beyond the other forms of public protest. Generally, it involves the protesters taking some degree of risk in order to highlight an issue.

This can range from risking prosecution for public order offences, to risking health by entering possibly dangerous situations. The aim is not, however, to take risks – it is to take action which directly confronts the issue, and highlights your cause, often dramatically. Careful planning should minimise the risks involved.

To achieve any form of public support, the protest should be carried out in a completely non-violent way.

Some examples of direct actions should illustrate the potential of this form of protest, and set you thinking about actions most suited to your campaign:-

- parents tired of calling for a pedestrian crossing in their community block the road and create their own at certain times of the day.

- residents concerned about health effects of a proposed mast in their area block access to the construction site.

- opponents of the pollution of a river block the outflow pipe of a company contributing to this pollution.

- a group of parents seeking a crèche at their place of work bring in their children on a chosen day.

- trees under threat are given a reprieve by protesters taking up residence in their branches.

- a multinational company could find its poor human rights record abroad highlighted by a group of protesters chained across the entrance to its head office here.

- a company selling weaponry to a country who would be likely to then use it against civilians could be targeted. Protesters could enter their premises and damage this equipment to protect possible victims. This was the case when in 1996 four women did £1.5m worth of damage to a Hawk aircraft in Britain which was part of a consignment for Indonesia. At the resulting court case the 'Ploughshares Four' successfully argued that they had used reasonable force to prevent a crime.

- a disabled lobby group protest poor access to a public building by creating a 'traffic jam' at its entrances.

In the environmental field, direct action forms the backbone of groups like Greenpeace and Earth First!, whose success is a measure of the effectiveness of such activity.

A more recent development in protesting is the idea of 'Culture Jamming'. This consists of altering the advertising of a target company, for instance, turning their marketing effort back against them. In other parts of the world Culture Jamming is used as an end in itself, but it also has potential as a campaign tool. Reproducing a company's ad and circulating it with some minor adjustments made to reverse the message, touching up a billboard with paints so that it tells the truth, and modifying the organisation's name wherever it is to be found, are some methods which have been used elsewhere.

A classic example of the work of a culture jammer would be a billboard ad for cigarettes, depicting galloping horses, with the message 'Do Horses Smoke?' sprayed across it.

By applying some thought and imagination it should be possible to adapt the tools of the Culture Jammer to many campaigns. If any proposed activities are illegal, the benefits and potential risks should be weighed up before proceeding.

Afterwards

Too often we miss some of our best learning opportunities – our mistakes.

- Have a debriefing session for all directly involved in the action as soon as possible afterwards, preferably straight away. At this you can discuss all practical aspects of the action and look at ways the next one could be improved, as well as celebrating what went well and getting in the first round of story telling!

- It is equally important for the Committee to get together a few days later to assess the effectiveness of the action in terms of media coverage, public perception and, most importantly, resulting campaign developments. In other words – Did it achieve what we wanted it to?

CAMPAIGN IMAGE AND MEDIA

It is very important that you consider the way your protest will be covered by the media at the earliest stages of planning. Whether your protest is a wild celebration of life through street theatre, or a strongly confrontational factory blockade, you want coverage to reflect your group's approach and campaign message, and this must be built in at all stages of the planning process.

Similarly, your protest should fit in with the campaign image, just like any of your other activities. The effect achieved by having a standard style and logo on banners and clothing during protests is well worth the effort.

(For more details on these issues, see Chapter 6: Promotion of the Group and Message, and Chapter 7: Working with the Media.)

HOW TO ORGANISE A MARCH OR RALLY

Initial Decisions

- What is the event calling for – Compensation Now! ? More Trees Please ? Give us back our Peace ?

- What will it be called – a Public March? A Protest Picnic? An Afternoon of Action?

- Do you want to organise it alone, or join forces with other groups?

- Decide on the date/route/other activities (face-painting music, provision of refreshments, clowns, street theatre?)

- Who do you want to attend? Targeting sections of the community should get the highest attendance for the lowest effort.

- Pick a target figure for attendance and work towards it.

- Try to estimate potential costs and get together a budget.

Organisation

- Gather a reliable organising group and decide on responsibilities. Share the work but make sure that it gets done.

- Pool your contacts and make out a list of people who can offer special help.

- Contact your local Gardaí to notify them of the event – hopefully they will provide an escort for a march. It is probably wise to organise your own stewards as well, to make sure that people don't stray or cause unnecessary disruption.

- Brainstorm slogans for banners and placards, and then have them made. A mixture of home-made and professional quality ones is best, and get the children to make their own.

- Prepare fliers and posters and send them to relevant organisations about two weeks beforehand. Organise a door-to-door drop in the relevant areas. Send a letter and poster to all active volunteers, encouraging them to bring more people with them. Maybe phone around the week before. Put posters up in local shops, schools, libraries, community centres, businesses, and so on. Put up large posters on lamp posts about four to five days beforehand.

- Contact the local media (newspaper and radio) to publicise the event, and inform the national media where appropriate.

- If you are having speakers, then you will probably need some form of Public Address system, or a megaphone. These are widely available for hire.

- If you plan to invite local politicians, an up-to-date list is available from your Local Authority.(See Chapter 9: Political Lobbying.)

- A couple of days before the event, send out a Press Notice to newsdesks and a Photo Opportunity Notice to Photo Editors in the relevant media, and follow them up with phone calls. On the day, send out a Press Release to the same people.

- And when all this is done – have fun!

HOW TO MAKE PLACARDS AND BANNERS

These are common tools of the trade for any kind of public protest, and are the most simple way to communicate a message to a number of people. For this reason, it is usually best to keep the message short and concise, something snappy that people will immediately understand and remember. If it is clever enough it could make a media image on its own.

Placards

A placard is usually a piece of stiff cardboard with writing on it. Making these up can be a lot of fun, as you can let loose the artist and the wit in you!

Tips:-

- Don't make the placard too flimsy as the Irish climate can turn it soggy and floppy very quickly. Use waterfast marking materials.

- If you don't have white cardboard use any colour and stick paper over it.

- Staple or tape it onto a lath or brush handle for extra height, a sandwich of cardboard with the handle up the middle makes a two-sided placard.

- Drawing it out on a scrap of paper first can save squeezing in words at the end.

- Make the words big enough to be read from a distance.

- A group of identical placards can be quite effective.

Banners

A banner is usually bigger and made from material. It can be used as a backdrop for speakers or a press conference, and is equally at home in a static or moving protest. In extreme cases they can be hung on bridges and buildings.

Banner making can be as simple or as elaborate as you want. A sheet tacked onto two brush handles with a freehand message painted on is quick and effective. However, a more carefully made banner can last longer and looks quite professional.

To make a 'proper' banner:-

- Decide on your message, then fiddle around with it on paper for a while in different formats. See what it would look like done out long and thin, or put on a square banner.

- The shape of the banner will be dictated by the message and the way it will be used, for instance long and thin is quite good at the front of a march or along a railing, while tall or square is a good backdrop for a speaker. If it is to be used outdoors, don't make it so big that it will act like a sail in high winds – it's no joke trying to keep it in one place.

- Having settled on a design, get your materials together – for the banner itself, try to use natural materials, such as the cheap and widely available unbleached calico. The same goes for paints – using emulsion rather than solvent based paint also makes it easier to clean your brushes. The combination of colours is important, particularly as most newspaper coverage will be black and white. Get a photographer to advise on this, but black on white or white on black are safe options.

- Someone handy with a sewing machine can make short work of a banner. Sew up the two ends to make sleeves to push poles through after measuring them to size. If you prefer, just reinforce the corners with a few thicknesses of cloth and put eyelets in them (kits available from boating suppliers and some hardware shops).

- For working on lettering, try to lay out the whole banner on a flat surface. Transfer your details from the paper onto the banner in pencil. When you are happy that it looks right, get on and fill in the letters. For a highly professional finish, the letters could be made from material and individually sewn on, but painting them in is much quicker and is perfectly acceptable (remember to put newspaper under the banner if you are painting it in your kitchen!). At this point everyone can join in, and a session of banner and placard making can be very enjoyable.

HOW TO PREPARE A DIRECT ACTION

This section is geared towards 'up front' actions which are non-violent, where the group is making its involvement clear and is willing to stand over its activities.

Initial Decisions

The decision to take direct action against a given target is an important one, and should only be made after careful consideration of the options. Direct action should only be used where it is the form of protest most likely to achieve results. Once the decision has been made, one person should be given responsibility for the action from beginning to end – the Action Co-ordinator. This person must come up with a number of options for the committee to select from.

Scouting

This is the information gathering stage, and good detective work will greatly improve the safety and chance of success of the action.

Preliminary scouting is required to enable the Action Co-ordinator to get some ideas together. This involves taking a look at all potential targets – for a polluting company they might check out all facilities of the company in the area, including offices.

With the decision taken on what the action should be, full scouting must then take place:-

- Scouting can be done blatantly by walking up to a target, taking photographs, stepping out measurements, and taking notes, but this is likely to draw attention, so it is usually better to pose as a bird watcher (hence the binoculars and camera which you might be carrying'), amateur botanist ('Oh sorry, I didn't realise I was on private property, but I thought I saw a rare spotted spineywort'), or some other suitable cover.

- Get to know the area around the target, and visit it at various times of the day to build up a full picture of the activities in the vicinity.

- Watch for security precautions such as cameras, lights, personnel and guard dogs.

Preparations

Once the group has decided on the action to be taken, the Action Co-ordinator makes the necessary preparations:-

- Draw up a detailed plan of what should happen on the day, determining what is required in terms of people, expertise, equipment, clothes, mobile phones and the logistics of getting it all together.

- Discuss the plan with the group's solicitor to determine what charges protesters could face in relation to their activities.

- Select the people to be involved, based on more than just availability. A 'soft' action might not require any great skills, but a 'hard' action would be more likely to be safe and effective if the participants work well as a team, are observant and not prone to over-reacting. It is essential that activists behave peacefully at all times, and only use passive resistance (passive resistance basically involves going limp, for instance if somebody tries to move you from the ground).

- Consider all the risks facing the protesters, and find ways to limit or eliminate them, whether by training, safety equipment, or modifications to the plan.

- Designate one person, preferably experienced, to take responsibility for safety and nothing else. This is a crucial task, and should be given to somebody who is observant and quick to react. They should also be trained in First Aid.

- Brief your Press Officer on the details of the action and discuss that side of things with them, including when to inform the media about the event, how much to tell them at first, and how to maximise coverage.

- Prepare participants for possible media interviews.

- Arrange your own stills and video photographers.

- Brief the participants on the background to the decision to do an action, the rationale for the action chosen, the details of what each person must do, and the legal implications. People need to know what charges they might face and the likely consequence, all of which should be explained by a solicitor who can then answer questions.

- For your own security it might be best to keep the details between as few people as possible until the last minute. It's a balance between trust and security and will be different from group to group, but it is a waste of time and effort when an action must be cancelled because of a careless comment overheard in public or on the phone, and care should be taken to prevent this.

- A final briefing (maybe also the first) of the activists should take place the night before, with everyone having the chance to clarify their roles, and even opt out if they don't feel comfortable with it. At the end of this briefing, the Action Co-ordinator should be happy that everything is set to go. People should prepare whatever warm clothes, food and equipment they need for the next day, and get a good night's sleep, although the last bit is easier said than done!

On the day

With all the preparations made there is nothing left to do but enjoy being at the cutting edge of your campaign and concentrate on getting the job done right.

- Meet at a designated point, such as the group's base or somewhere near the target, in plenty of time and do one final check to see that everything is in order. At this stage if there has been any change in the makeup of the group, the target, or even the weather, which could make the action unsafe, then don't be afraid to pull out – a good Action Co-ordinator must know where to draw the line.

- The adrenaline will be pumping, but care should be taken to keep everyone calm at all times and keep tension down so that nobody loses the head.

- Do It!

- During the action the Co-ordinator must know what is going on at all times and call the shots to keep everything in line. The Safety Co-ordinator should be standing back and watching for any form of risk, including unexpected ones which could need a quick response to avoid injury or damage.

- The end of the action needs to be clear – either by achieving the objective, or when the media coverage is likely to have been maximised, when concessions have been made by the target and so on. At this stage, pack up your gear and move off.

ANECDOTE: THE CAVAN POTHOLER

In 1988, fed up with local and national government apathy, Martin Hannigan decided to do something about the treacherous state of the roads in County Cavan. Within six months, there were five action groups up and running throughout the county.

These groups' initial strategy consisted of political lobbying – at both local and national level.

That didn't get them very far, however. The only response to their continuous questioning and requests was: 'no money'. They held huge protests and rallies, with great public turnouts and support. Four of their members were even elected to local government in the last local elections, such was the support of the people. Still no result. The roads were as dangerous as ever. Politics just was not working for them. Lives were at risk from the state of the roads and they could do nothing about it.

After three years of knocking their heads against a brick wall, the groups began to fall apart, disillusioned with the lack of progress in the campaign, despite all of the hard work that had been put in. So, armed with his can of fluorescent paint, Martin decided to continue with the struggle – on his own if necessary. Talking hadn't worked. It seemed to Martin as though it was now time to commence a more direct form of action.

Things really seemed to take off in 1991, when he began to paint fluorescent circles around the potholes on the Cavan roads. Highlighting the problem with paint seemed the only solution after so little political success. To Martin's surprise, this action attracted media attention from as far away as the United States. Closer to home, Sky News and Terry Wogan covered the story as did RTÉ, both television and radio. Newspaper headlines, both local and national read.... 'Our Councillors Don't Care' and 'Cavan Roads of Shame'.

This media attention brought with it a fair measure of success. A film crew which informed the local authority of their plans to make a documentary on the campaign got more than they bargained for. When they returned with their cameras, the particularly bad stretch of road they had planned to film had been miraculously repaired overnight. VIP visits have also been known to spark similar repairs.

Martin Hannigan's actions in highlighting these dangerous potholes gets the message across to the public and those in power.

It is having an effect on the situation and has also encouraged others in a similar situation to get up and do something about it.
'Paint is a very easy way of delivering a message.'

9
POLITICAL LOBBYING

'A diplomat ... is a person who can tell you to go to hell in such a way that you actually look forward to the trip.'

Cassie Stinnett, American writer.

'Action comes from keeping the heat on. No politician can sit on a hot issue if you make it hot enough.'

Saul Alinsky, Radical organiser and author.

INTRODUCTION

We elect politicians, and they are answerable to us. They are our representatives and good campaign groups acknowledge and make use of this fact.

All political lobbying involves knowing three things, the politicians, the system and how they fit into it. While the Dáil is the system that people are most familiar with, groups can also lobby on a range of fronts including local and European bodies.

This chapter aims to explain the political routes into these centres of decision-making. It gives advice on how to convince politicians that your campaign is worth supporting, and that it is in their political interest to do so.

WHAT POLITICIANS CAN DO FOR YOU

The benefits of having some politicians on your side can be quite significant.

They might have the power to bring about change themselves. If not, they can bring your issue to the attention of relevant ministers or civil servants, and can use their influence within their own political body. They can source information and answers which you might have difficulty in getting on your own. They can help with bringing your issue to outside bodies, such as the European Commission.

The support of a politician is also important in lending credibility to your campaign. This can help to increase public support and improve your chances of obtaining media coverage. (See Appendix for information on political structures.)

Local Politicians

Local Authority Councillors

Your Local Councillor can bring your issue to the attention of the rest of the Council, and make sure that it is appropriately aired at their meetings. They can arrange for a deputation from your group to be received by the Council, although due to time constraints this is not very common. They can also table motions of endorsement and support for your cause within the Council, which can carry weight within the Local Authority system and central government.

The next level in a Local Authority is made up of Committees. A Councillor can ensure that your issue is tabled and discussed by the relevant Committee. They can also arrange for your admittance to the public gallery to view Committee meetings.

The support of a Councillor, or better still, a number of Councillors can help in arranging meetings with officials of the Local Authority. If possible, get your Councillors to attend these meetings as well, so that they can keep an eye on how your issue is being handled.

National Politicians

TDs

An effective and hard-working TD has quite a few routes through which to highlight an issue nationally. They can put a good word in the appropriate Minister's ear (the value of such a tactic should not be underestimated!). They can help to organise meetings between representatives of your group and the appropriate politician. They can also use a number of parliamentary devices which are outlined below: –

Dáil Questions

- Oral Questions. Dáil Deputies can ask questions of the Government relating to public or administrative matters. These have to be addressed specifically to the Government Department with responsibility for the issue raised.

Deputies can only ask each Minister two questions on any sitting day. Five can be nominated for priority each day. These are allocated between parties, based on Party strengths. Oral questions must be submitted four days in advance.

In suggesting a question to a TD, you should make sure that it is clear and concise. The more tightly worded the question, the better your chance of having it asked, and maybe even getting a useful answer.

- Private Notice Questions

  The Ceann Comhairle can accept questions relating to matters of urgent public importance at short notice. These are taken at the end of Question Time.

- Written Questions

  Deputies can also present questions for written reply to Government members. These are useful for gathering facts and highlighting your campaign.

  Any number of written questions can be asked. The more tabled on your behalf by different politicians the better, as this gives an indication of the extent of public concern.

Letters to Ministers

While a letter from your group may not get to the Minister's desk, every letter written by a TD will be read and responded to by the Minister. Again, it is to your advantage to have as many TDs as possible writing on your behalf, to show the level of support for your issue.

Adjournment Debates

TDs may be able to present your case in an adjournment debate, which is the last item of each day in the Dáil. Here a Member gets the opportunity to speak for fifteen minutes (or decides to share this time with other Deputies), and the relevant Minister replies for the same length of time, putting the Government's case forward.

Party Whips

In advance of Dáil sittings on Tuesdays, party groups usually meet to decide party positions on upcoming issues. It is useful to lobby for your issue to be brought up at these meetings.

Each party will have a representative, called a whip. The whip will represent the party line when they all meet together, usually on Thursday mornings, to discuss the business for the following week. You can lobby them directly, and through their party colleagues. It is worthwhile to lobby a different party whip each week to keep your item on the agenda until it is dealt with.

Parliamentary Committees

Both the Dáil and Seanad have the power to form Special or Select Committees for particular purposes. A Joint Committee consists of members from both Houses.

Your TD or Senator can ensure that your point of view is represented at this forum, or better still that you get a chance to make a presentation to the Committee.

Committee powers can include the following: –

- Receiving submissions, or hearing evidence from interested groups or individuals.

- Discussing and drafting proposals for legislative change.

- Publishing of minutes of evidence and related documents.

- Requesting the attendance of Ministers to discuss current policies, or proposals for legislation.

Senators

Having the support of a Senator is likely to help the public profile of the campaign. In addition to lending credibility, they can seek further assistance for your group from their Dáil colleagues.

If your campaign includes trying to influence some piece of legislation, the backing of a Senator can prove very useful. After a Bill has been through a Committee or the Dáil, it goes to the Seanad. Lobby Senators to introduce amendments at this stage. The Bill will then pass back to the Dáil.

As explained in the previous section, Senators can also be involved in various Parliamentary Committees.

Ministers

Providing that the governing parties (or party) hold a satisfactory majority, no Bill will be passed without the support of the government. This means that lobbying of the government, both directly and through other politicians, is vital to many campaigns.

This is where the power lies, and this is where you must focus pressure in order to achieve campaign goals.

Your political route into the process is via the Taoiseach and Ministers, or their Special Advisors and Programme Managers.

Ministers are also very involved in other decisions of political or strategic importance. If you feel it is appropriate to your campaign, try your hardest to get a face-to-face meeting using any political or other influence possible.

And, remember, Ministers are politicians who will have to face their electorate again, just like other TDs and Local Councillors. Therefore, it is up to campaign groups to show the level of public support for their issue and to help push issues into positions of political or strategic importance.

European Politicians

MEPs

While it will take patience and persistence to get the active backing of a Member of the European Parliament, they should be contacted at the early stages of your campaign. Through their office they will advise you on how to take your issue through the political structures of the European Union, and whether it is useful for your group to do so.

The two main routes which they are likely to suggest are making a complaint to the European Commission, and sending a petition to the European Parliament.

If you suspect that EU regulations have been breached, you should lodge a complaint with the relevant department (Directorate General) of the European Commission in Brussels. If your complaint is judged by the Commission to be legitimate, it has to investigate and request information about what remedial action is being taken by the Irish authorities.

The assistance of an MEP is more important when it comes to sending a petition to the European Parliament. This course of action is one of the few sources of real access which individual citizens have to the Parliament as an institution. It is useful in that representatives of other institutions, particularly the Commission, can be called to attend meetings and give details of what action they have taken on certain petitions. MEPs can press the Commission for more detailed information if necessary, and can speak out against any shortcomings in the way that petitions are being handled.

MEPs can also table one oral question to the Commission, and one to the Council of Ministers each month. The usefulness of having your campaign issue raised in this way has more to do with the level at which it is aired and the resulting political pressure at home than with the response itself. It is a good idea to get at least two cross-party MEP's on your side as this can politically influence Commissioners.

Finally, EU institutions thrive on bureaucracy. If you feel that your matter is not being dealt with satisfactorily, despite your firmness and patience, then you should contact your MEP.

LOBBYING STRATEGY

The strategy you take in relation to political lobbying will very much depend on the type of campaign you are running, and in particular, whether it is publicly acceptable or not.

You may be campaigning on an issue which already has the support of some or all of the local politicians, or you might have built up good relations with them from past activities. In such cases the political door will already be partly open. On the other hand if the issue is divisive, then you will have plenty of lobbying to do!

Identify your Targets

The first step in the lobbying process is to work out whom you need to focus on.

- Identify which constituency you are in, and which Local Authority administers your area.

- Clarify which Councillors, and sub-committees, if any, are relevant. You can get a list from your Local Authority office. They will also tell you which Councillors are members of what Committees.

- Decide which local and/or national TD's you want to focus on. A full list is available from the Public Relations Office in Leinster House.

- Clarify which Minister and Ministers of State have responsibilities relating to your issue.

- Identify the relevant party spokespeople and the names of each party whip.

- If you feel your issue can be dealt with by the EU, find out the names of the relevant MEPs and Directorate Generals from the European Parliament Office.

Remember, don't become too aligned with a minority political party. Try to get broad support, particularly from the larger parties. This should prevent your issue from becoming marginalised.

When the above is clarified, compile a mailing list of the relevant people, including contact addresses and phone numbers. Like your media list, this will become dog-eared and invaluable as the campaign progresses.

Build up your credibility

Before you approach the politicians, particularly if yours is a local campaign, it is advisable to do a bit of grass-roots work first. Spread the word locally, distribute your leaflets, get some media coverage, gather signatures and compile a list of supporting organisations, residents' groups and patrons. That way when you approach the politicians, it is clear that you are not just a bunch of nutters, but rather an organised group already attracting a certain amount of credibility and support.

Encourage the Public to Express their Opinions

From the beginning, you should be encouraging your supporters and members of the public to write to your target politicians themselves. They should give their personal views and express support for the aims of your campaign. A draft letter and contact addresses can be printed on all your leaflets. (See Chapter 6: Promotion of the Group and Message.)

Encourage people to attend TDs' clinics to verbally express their views. It is very important that politicians are made aware in as many ways as possible that their constituents, or potential Party voters are extremely concerned about the situation.

Inform Politicians of your Campaign and Request Initial Meeting

Send a letter to each politician on your mailing list outlining the aims of your campaign, including a copy of your campaign leaflet and any other informational material. Ask them for a meeting in which you wish to discuss the issues relating to your campaign and to solicit their views. If you do not receive an early response, follow up the letter with a phone call.

Don't be put off if the relevant politicians are not too keen to meet you at first. As the campaign gains momentum, try again, and they may then see the importance of direct communication.

Organise your own Political Lobbying Meetings

At various stages in the campaign, you may want to arrange meetings in your office, or campaign base. The aim here would be to update the relevant politicians, or solicit their assistance on some recent development. If you wish to do this, try to send or fax an invitation to them at least a week in advance of the meeting date. Follow this up with a phone call, to check whether they can come, and if they are unable to attend, request that someone else be sent in their place.

If you are targeting Dáil TDs from various constituencies (say the party spokespeople on a particular issue), then schedule the meeting for midweek, in Dublin, at a venue near the Dáil. That way you can nab them while they are all in the one place for Dáil business.

Request a Meeting with the Relevant Minister

If this step is appropriate to your campaign, make a detailed submission to the Minister, enclosing any background information, and ask for a meeting. Follow up with a phone call.

Keep Politicians Informed

Don't forget to keep the relevant politicians informed of your activities, and the progress of the campaign. Send them any new leaflets, newsletters, reports or other useful sources of information. Even if they are not used at the time, these will be put on file and may come in handy for future reference.

If you feel it is appropriate, invite them to your public meetings and other major events.

Announce your Own Political Candidate

If you want to apply more political pressure, you may want to think about putting up your own candidate in the next Local or General Election. You would be surprised how an announcement of this intention will make politicians react, particularly those who know that their seats are a little wobbly. As well as garnering the votes of your supporters, your candidate would also presumably attract some 'rebel', 'anti-party' or other floating voters, creating a force to be reckoned with.

If you go down this route, don't just make an idle threat. You must be sure that you will be able to produce a keen candidate if or when the election looms, and that your group will be in a position to supply all the energy, stamina and funding needed to run an impressive pre-election campaign. A half-hearted threat, or even worse, a half-baked electoral campaign, will only damage the determined image of your group, and could cast doubts on its credibility.

When choosing your candidate, try to get someone who, as well as taking your issue on board, will have knowledge and views on other subjects. Ideally, the person should have a flair for public speaking and a good understanding, if not experience, of the political process.

PETITIONS

A petition is a collection of signatures about a particular issue. It is a good campaign tool which can display the level of support for your aims to relevant politicians and decision-makers in business or other organisations.

Collecting a petition has a number of potential benefits:-

- The signatures can be sent to the decision-maker as evidence of the wealth of support behind the campaign.

- A large petition can show that your issue has voting power. In a local constituency, 10,000 signatures can unsettle politicians and encourage them to take your campaign seriously. In an election, that number of voters could threaten one seat, at least.

- Looking for signatures of support is also a great way of testing the waters. What do the people think? At times in a campaign, you can feel quite isolated and demoralised, but when you hit the streets you may be surprised by the level of support which actually exists 'out there'.

- The process of talking to people and answering their questions gives you a great opportunity to hone down the arguments of the campaign, and to understand what information people want. No doubt, you will meet some opponents, so you can keep on top of their arguments and learn how best to respond.

Tips

- If you are unlikely to get a large number of signatures, it is probably better to get people to write individual letters instead. These can be similarly effective in showing decision-makers the depth of feeling people have about the campaign. Such letters must be answered individually.

- Handing over the petition can be turned into an event in itself, further focusing attention on your campaign message.

HOW TO GET THE MOST FROM POLITICAL LOBBYING MEETINGS

The Meeting Itself

- Check in advance how much time is allotted for the meeting, so that you can plan the length of your presentation.

- Be clear on the purpose of the meeting, what points you want to cover, what you want the politician to do and what you want to achieve.

  It's usually good if three or four people attend and each one takes on a pre-arranged role. For instance, one could act as leader, explaining the reason for the meeting, introducing everyone and making sure each has their say. Others could have specific points to bring up, while another takes notes. One could take an aggressive, pushy approach, while another acts as placator. The position of note-taker is very important as the notes can be typed up later, used for future reference on what was said or promised, and distributed to members who did not attend.

- You should meet for at least half an hour before the proposed meeting to refresh your memories and to rehearse your case or presentation for the final time.

- Do not leave without clarifying what position the politician is taking on the issue and what they intend to do. Remember, the aim of all lobbying is to encourage positive action, not just to have amiable chats. After the meeting, send a thank-you letter, outlining the actions you believe they have promised to undertake. Offer to meet again in the future, or to send on further information, should the need arise.

Briefing Documents

- It is important that you send any information leaflets or reports relating to your campaign in advance of the meeting, so that the politicians have a chance to inform themselves.

- It is also advisable to prepare a short briefing paper, which should explain who you are and summarise the campaign's aims and main arguments in a coherent, point-by-point format. Be clear on what you want done. Avoid jargon and unnecessary statistics. This document can either be sent in advance, or given to them at the meeting. Its main purpose is to provide a record of your case, written in your own terms. Otherwise, politicians will rely on their notes of your arguments.

- Remember that by informing and briefing your politicians adequately, you are saving them and everyone else a lot of time.

Other Points

- If possible, try to ensure that the same lobbying team attends all or most of the meetings. That way you can ensure continuity, and politicians' responses can be contrasted and compared.

- Depending on your strategy, you may want to include statements made by the politician in your next leaflet, or newsletter, or to include them immediately in a press release to the media. Inform the politicians if using their statements.

- It's best to try and arrange to meet TDs in their Dáil offices, rather than their clinics, as this will give the meeting greater importance. However, if you live outside of Dublin, this may not be practical.

- While deputations at Council meetings are not very frequent, it's worth asking the Cathaoirleach if you can make a presentation. Before doing so, ensure that you have cultivated a few Councillors, so that you will have some friendly support in the Chamber. Presenting your case in this way saves time, as rather than meeting with each Councillor separately, you will hit a group of them together. However, you do miss out on the personal trust-building approach, so it is best to combine the two tactics.

- TDs have no formal influence on the Local Authority in which their constituency is situated. However, even if your issue is very local, and doesn't warrant legislative change, having TDs on your side is extremely important, particularly when they act as advocates on your behalf. Don't forget, some TDs are also Councillors and all know that their votes come from local constituencies, so they are very much affected by your opinions. Besides, many 'local' issues can become 'national' if your campaign harnesses enough media attention, and generates a lot of public support or controversy.

- Depending on your campaign, it may be very difficult to secure a meeting with the relevant Minister. The act of formally meeting with you demonstrates an implicit recognition of your concerns which may draw criticism from the Opposition. If you feel it is important to your campaign, don't give up. Try every avenue possible – get friendly TDs, Senators and other influential people to put a word in for you and meet with the Programme Managers, or Advisors. If all else fails, you could always turn up outside one of their Official Engagements!

- If approaching MEPs for a meeting, be aware that they are abroad a lot. You may have to make arrangements well in advance, or meet at very short notice.

HOW TO ORGANISE PETITIONS

In Advance

Decide on the targets of the petition – whom will you send it to? who do you want to sign it? from what area?

Set a date for completion, and set a target number of signatures so that you have something to work towards.

Work out the wording for the petition carefully. This statement is what people will be agreeing to support, so you should make it clear and concise.

Type up a master copy on a computer and make photocopies as you need them.

Work out a plan of action – deciding where and when you will gather the signatures.

Options:

- A door-to-door knock.

- Standing outside central points such as town/village squares, shopping centres, churches, the local park, beach, or sports grounds.

- Collecting at campaign specific sites – for instance, focusing on the users of the service or amenity which you are campaigning to preserve.

Organise rotas so that people are not left at the job for more than two hours at a time. Anything over this can be really hard work, particularly if it's cold.

Prepare your volunteers, especially if they are new to the campaign, by organising a question and answer role play session. At this, you can practise the best way to ask for signatures, how to explain the campaign, and answer common or difficult questions.

Make sure that each petitioner is armed with a clip board, signature sheets and a pen. Supply them with information leaflets for people who want to know more and a sheet on which to sign up any new volunteers.

On the Day

Make sure that the public know at a glance what you are doing. If the campaign name is not visible they will often presume you are selling lines, and do their best to avoid you. You could wear your campaign T-shirts/sweat-shirts (if you have them), make visible tags for your lapels, or put a large slogan on the back of the petition board and hold this up. If you are standing at one spot, you could erect sandwich boards, displaying your campaign logo or slogan, and asking people to sign.

It is always best to petition in twos, or larger teams if you are trying to blitz an area. Working with other people is safer, as well as more fun. If someone is nasty, you at least have a friend to laugh it over with! Make sure that at least one experienced campaigner is in each team, to offer advice to new volunteers, and to deal with any of the more complex questions.

Try not to get cornered by people who just want to give out about the campaign. There is no point in wasting valuable signature-collecting time by arguing with someone whose view you will be unlikely to change.

Lastly, go forth and multiply!

ANECDOTE: TRÓCAIRE / OGONI JOINT OIREACHTAS COMMITTEE

During the past three years, Trócaire, the Catholic Agency for World Development, has consistently worked at highlighting the human rights and environmental abuses in Nigeria under the present regime. Together with other solidarity, environmental and human rights groups, Trócaire staged a number of demonstrations and vigils outside the Nigerian Embassy during the cold November evenings leading up to and following the execution of Ken Saro-Wiwa and the other Ogoni activists in 1995.

While the world expressed its outrage, the EU agreed to modest sanctions and the Commonwealth threatened to expel Nigeria from the club. The spotlight soon left Nigeria and the media moved on to cover the next story. However, Trócaire was committed to staying with the issue and produced a number of position papers including recommendations for action and presented them to key politicians. The campaigns officer asked for permission to brief the Joint Oireachtas Committee on Foreign Affairs on the situation in Nigeria following the executions and presented a proposed resolution for adoption to the committee on 29 November. There was some reluctance to support the call for an oil embargo and other strong measures on that occasion and it was clear that some convincing needed to be done. In the months that followed Trocaire continued to feed information and analysis to the Committee both through the Chairperson, Alan Dukes and individual sympathetic members. And on being invited back again before the Committee on 17 January the Committee unanimously passed a resolution put forward by Jim O Keefe which:

- 'Condemns the regime in Nigeria for the hanging of Ken Saro-Wiwa and eight other Ogoni activists on Friday, 10 November, 1995;

- Demands a fair trial, by normal judicial process, for the Ogonis still detained, with independent observers present at the trial;

- Calls on the Government to press for the imposition of sanctions on the regime at EU and UN levels and, in particular, to seek the introduction of an oil embargo and the freezing of assets of the current military regime held in foreign bank accounts; further calls on the Government to support such other steps as will be taken by the international community to bring about the replacement of the present military dictatorship in Lagos with a fully democratically elected Government; questions the role of Shell Oil in continuing to co-operate with the present regime in Nigeria and invites a representative from the company to come before the Committee to explain it; and requests the Ambassador of Nigeria to attend before the Committee at its next meeting.'

The following month Mr Achebe, General Manger of Shell Nigeria, was invited before the Committee to answer questions regarding Shell's continued co-operation with the present regime. Ireland became the first country to call Shell before a parliamentary committee to answer criticisms. This event has greatly encouraged people on the ground in Nigeria who are struggling to peacefully restore democracy and human rights in their country.

Annette Honan, Campaigns Officer, Trócaire.

10
LEGAL AND PLANNING ISSUES

'When it comes to the future, there are three kinds of people: those who let it happen, those who make it happen and those who wonder what happened.'

Anonymous

INTRODUCTION

In Ireland we have a tradition of mistrusting the authorities, going back hundreds of years. These days however, people are less shy about becoming involved in the legal system, and campaign groups are no exception.

While it is no short cut to success, it is fair to say that the number of campaign groups achieving the desired result through legal action is high enough to warrant attention. Many approaches, from simple injunctions to major appeals in the European courts, have been successfully used as campaign tools.

The aim of this chapter is to set out in plain language the important elements of the legal and planning systems. There is no danger that you will have become a solicitor at the end of it, but hopefully you will have a grounding in the subject. This should be enough for you to consider legal action as a way of advancing your campaign, up to the point of getting in professional help.

THE COURT SYSTEM – STRUCTURE

There are four levels of court in the Irish system, each with its own jurisdiction. There is a clear line of appeal up through the courts, ending with the Supreme Court. Cases can also be referred or appealed to the European Courts. We will look at these, beginning with the lowest and working our way up.

District Court

This court has limited jurisdiction and deals chiefly with 'minor matters'. These include motoring offences, taxation and insurance irregularities, licencing applications and certain local government issues. The District Court does not deal with serious crime, libel or slander cases, or the granting of injunctions.

The maximum amount which can be pursued or awarded for damages stands at £5,000.

The District Court tends to be a solicitors' court and will rarely involve the use of a barrister, a barrister being a more specialist advocate. This means that proceedings will be relatively inexpensive (as opposed to cheap!). Another advantage is that this court tends to be speedier than the others.

Sittings of the Court are usually held at least once a month in each District Court area or large town.

A person may only be sued in the area where they live or carry on business, or in the area where the offence took place.

Circuit Court

This court has greater powers than the District Court. Some of the business consists of hearing appeals from the District Court.

When suing for damages here the maximum amount recoverable is £30,000.

Cases will usually involve the use of a barrister, which can add to the expense. Also, in many parts of the country there can be a considerable delay in getting a Circuit Court case on for hearing.

Circuits are organised on a regional basis, usually by county.

High Court

This is the highest court at which proceedings can begin. It deals with the trial of serious offences such as murder, and is the usual court of application for injunctions. (Though they can be obtained in the Circuit Court.) The High Court hears appeals from the Circuit Court, as well as applications for the judicial review of decisions of various bodies such as An Bord Pleanála. (Judicial Reviews are covered in a later section.)

Most cases will involve the use of barristers and tend to be expensive. There is also a significant backlog of cases, although urgent ones can be brought to trial quite quickly.

Usually cases will be heard in Dublin, but the Court does go on circuit to some of the bigger urban centres once or twice a year.

Supreme Court

This is the highest court in the Irish system, but it does not hear any cases at first instance. Instead its role is to hear appeals from the High Court or cases referred from other courts. This will only happen where there is a point of law, as opposed to fact, involved.

Appeals to the Supreme Court can be expensive.

An additional role of the Supreme Court is to judge the constitutionality of any proposed legislation referred to it by the President.

In some circumstances the Supreme Court can refer cases to the European Court of Justice because of a possible conflict with European Community Law.

European Courts of Justice

These only interact with our judicial system when an element of a case before our courts involves a matter of European Law which cannot be resolved by domestic Irish Law.

THE COURT SYSTEM – PROCEDURE

There are a number of routes available to a campaign group wishing to take legal action. The following are the main options, including the basics on how to go about them.

Bringing a Case

District Court

Bringing a civil case to the District Court involves an initiating document called a Civil Process, which contains basic information on the parties involved and the Endorsement of Claim. The Endorsement of Claim will show how much is being claimed, why it is being claimed, and include a claim for costs. This document sets the whole process in motion and will usually be served on the defendant by registered post.

Criminal cases or prosecutions are initiated by a summons, which is processed in a similar way to the Civil Process.

Circuit Court

Here, the initiating document in a civil claim is called a Civil Bill. In Circuit Court proceedings the matter involved may be referred to a barrister for their advice. They will also assist with drawing up the Endorsement of Claim and preparing the case for trial.

High Court

The initiating document is a Summons, and this will include an Endorsement of Claim with a general description of the plaintiffs claim – the plaintiff being the party taking the action. After the defendant has entered an Appearance with the High Court, a document stating that they will turn up and contest the case, a detailed Statement of Claim is sent to them by the plaintiff. A Defence may then be entered. A Notice for Trial will be sent by the plaintiff, which will place the case into a list of forthcoming cases in chronological order depending on when they were set down for trial. The delay in getting from the bottom to the top of the list can be considerable – sometimes years.

Bases for legal action

Some of the bases for taking action include:-

* Nuisance – unreasonable interference with somebody's rights, often to property and usually on an ongoing basis.

* Negligence – this is where the opposition had a duty of care, there was a breach of that duty, and this resulted in loss or damage which was reasonably foreseeable.

* Rule in Rylands v Fletcher – this case established a precedent, allowing action to be taken where there is an escape of something from one person's land to another, other than from natural use of the land, and damage can be shown to have happened as a result. It is a form of strict or 'no fault' liability, meaning that there is no need to show negligence or intention to cause harm.

Judicial Review

This remedy involves the High Court reviewing a decision made usually by a public body. If a person feels that a body or organisation has not invoked the correct procedures in coming to its decision it can apply to the High Court for a Judicial Review. This could result in the decision being overturned.

It is a fundamental principle of our system of justice that parties affected by any decision be afforded what is known as 'natural justice'. Two important elements of this concept are; that in every instance a person must be afforded the opportunity to present their case; and that a person may only be tried in accordance with the law.

Thus, in reaching a decision on a case coming before it, if, for example, An Bord Pleanála or the Law Society do not follow the correct procedure under the law, they would be leaving the avenue open to an aggrieved party to seek a judicial review of their decision.

The High Court can only interfere if the procedure is shown to have been flawed. It cannot substitute its own view on the facts of the case.

Injunction

This is a Court order requiring a party to do, or to refrain from doing, something. It is usually sought as a matter of urgency when something is going to happen imminently.

Usually the procedure is that an application is made for an Interim Injunction until a further trial of the matter. The idea here is to preserve the situation as it exists until the time of the trial. In these circumstances, the party seeking the injunction must give an undertaking to the court to pay damages, in case the injunction is granted but then withdrawn when it comes to court for a full hearing.

By its nature the initial application for an injunction will usually be *ex parte*, or without the other side knowing. It will include an Affidavit, or sworn statement in writing, setting out the reasons for the application. On receipt of these papers, the Court Office passes them on to a judge and directs the applicant to appear in court. It is a requirement that the party should be frank in its disclosures to the court, even if it may weaken the case, since the other party is not given an opportunity to put its side of the case at this time.

The interim injunction will usually only last for a short period of a couple of days to a week. This is to allow the other side to come to court to give its side of the story as soon as possible. This next stage is known as an Interlocutory Hearing. At this hearing, an interlocutory injunction will be granted if the judge still feels that the injunction should be continued until the full hearing of the action (which may be some months away).

It is possible to obtain an injunction at any time when the situation is urgent. In exceptional circumstances, such as if the court is not sitting or it is the middle of the night, the application can be made at the judge's home or any convenient location. This will be done through a barrister, and the plaintiff will usually be present. The injunction will then be awarded for the shortest possible time (an interim injunction) to enable notice to be served on the Defendants for the interlocutory hearing.

If the situation is not urgent, then there may be no need for an interim injunction, and the whole procedure will start off at the interlocutory hearing stage.

Some injunctions will last indefinitely from the date on which they are granted, and these are known as Perpetual Injunctions. Others can be for a specific date or event.

Injunctions can be a very effective remedy in some situations. However, they can also be costly, and carry an element of risk due to the undertaking as to damages.

Appeals

The appeal process is normally quite straightforward – District Court cases can be appealed to the Circuit Court, Circuit Court cases to the High Court. In both circumstances a Notice of Appeal must be served on the other side within a specified period after the court hearing. When a case is appealed, it is usually completely re-heard in the same way as an ordinary case commenced in that court.

A case may only be heard on appeal by the Supreme Court where a point of law or a constitutional issue is involved.

THE PLANNING SYSTEM – STRUCTURE

At its simplest, the Local Authority grants planning permission, and An Bord Pleanála deals with appeals.

Role of Local Authority

In its role as the planning authority, the Local Authority has the following functions:-

- To make, review, and implement a Development Plan.
- To decide on planning applications in accordance with: –
  – proper planning and development of the area.

- provisions of the development plan.
- any orders covering special amenity areas.

- To decide on whether to take legal action where planning permission was not granted but development went ahead, or where conditions have not been followed.

- To decide whether to pay compensation in certain instances where permission has been refused or restrictive conditions have been imposed.

It is also bound to keep a planning register available for public inspection. This will contain any planning decisions it makes.

A planning authority cannot grant permission which effectively contradicts its development plan, unless the procedure prescribed under the law is followed. The authority must publish a notice of its intention in a newspaper relevant to that locality, and then pass a resolution to that effect among its elected members.

With any permission, the authority can impose conditions, both financial and structural. There must be a reasonable connection between the conditions and the proposed development.

Role of An Bord Pleanála (The Planning Board)

The basic function of the Board is to deal with appeals from any interested parties following a decision to grant, refuse, or attach conditions to a permission by a planning authority.

Unlike the planning authority itself, the Board has the power to grant planning permission for a development which is expressly contrary to the development plan. It must have regard to the provisions of the development plan, but it is not legally obliged to give effect to its terms.

It has the power to request any documentation which it considers relevant from any parties to an appeal. Under the rules of natural justice, each side must be given the opportunity to respond to any submissions made or documents lodged by the other side.

It can take into account matters not raised by the parties, but they must then be informed of this and given an opportunity to comment. The Board can specify that a permission last for more than five years. It is bound, under statute, to keep itself informed about the policies of government, Local Authorities and any other body which has a bearing on planning and development, such as the ESB, Telecom, An Post and Bord Fáilte.

In considering an appeal, a member of the Board can enter on the land in question at any reasonable time for any purpose connected with the appeal.

THE PLANNING SYSTEM – PROCEDURE

The planning system is set up in such a way that extensive involvement of the public is encouraged. There is scope for people and groups to submit comments at most stages of the process, beginning with the development plan of the Local Authority.

More details of the following procedures can be found in a series of Planning Leaflets available from your Local Authority and the Department of the Environment. There is a recent booklet published by Forbairt outlining the procedures.

Application Procedure

For most developments of land or property, planning permission is required from the planning authority (Local Authority). In addition to building, this includes demolition, alteration and significant changes in the use of land or buildings.

Where planning permission is required, public notice must be given, both in a local newspaper and in a notice on the site itself. Detailed maps and specifications must be submitted to the authority who will then pass copies to various interested parties, such as the local fire officer, and ask them for comment. It will then issue a decision, indicating its intention to issue a final grant of permission. Interested parties may then appeal that decision to An Bord Pleanála within one month. If no appeal is taken, a final grant of permission will be issued to the applicant.

In most cases a planning permission lasts for five years from the date on which it was granted, and must be acted upon within that time or it will lapse. Where a development has been commenced, the permission may be extended.

Commenting on an Application

Campaign groups, like individuals, are entitled to view any application for planning permission. They should be aware of the application from the notices mentioned above. They are also entitled to comment on it, even if not directly affected by it.

Comments on the application can be made to the planning authority at any time before a decision has been made. The authority must take all written comments into account, but only in so far as they are based on planning considerations.

This process offers groups the chance to not just express their opinion on an application for planning permission, but have it taken into account. If this is not successful you might consider the next step – taking an appeal.

Appealing a Planning Decision

Any legal person, including a group, can appeal any decision of a planning authority. This appeal must be in writing and should be sent directly to An Bord Pleanála, along with the appropriate fee, within one month of the decision. It must give a detailed account of the reasons on which it is founded in order to be valid. The appeal should also be accompanied by any documents or other information appropriate to the case. The time limit of one month is strictly enforced.

The appellant, the party bringing the appeal, cannot make further submissions unless requested to do so by the Board, so the original appeal documentation must be comprehensive and cover all areas of objection.

Any number of parties can appeal a grant of planning permission. Each party must be given a copy of every other appeal as soon as it has been received by the Board, and may then comment on it. If no such submission is made by them, then the Board can determine the appeal without further notice to that party.

It is worth noting that legal persons, who are not part of an appeal, can submit observations to the Board.

Once an appeal has been made, the applicant and the planning authority automatically become parties to it. However, if the Board is of the opinion that the appeal is of a frivolous nature, it can dismiss it.

The Board will appoint one of its inspectors to investigate and prepare a report on the appeal.

The Inspector's Report and Oral Hearings

The appeals process would normally be dealt with by the Inspector reviewing the various reports and submissions. The Board then takes a decision based upon the Inspector's report. However, parties, including campaign groups, can seek an oral hearing of the appeal. This involves elements of the appeal being heard at a public hearing. This heightens public awareness of the issues, which can be beneficial to a campaign group.

Application for an oral hearing must be made within one month of the planning decision. For this, a fee must be paid in addition to the fee for the appeal. The submission must state the full grounds of appeal. The Board has full discretion to refuse to hold an oral hearing (in which event the fee will be refunded), but will normally grant one where significant issues of public interest are involved.

The procedure with an oral hearing is that the Board must inform each of the parties of the time and place of the hearing at least seven days in advance. Such hearings are always held under the stewardship of the Inspector, who has a general discretion as to the conduct of the hearing, but it will not normally involve undue formality. They may allow parties to appear in person or be represented by others.

Regardless of whether there is an oral hearing, the Inspector has the power to:-

- Require an officer of the planning authority to provide any information deemed relevant to the appeal.

- Personally visit the land concerned.

- Engage consultants or advisors if deemed necessary.

- Refer any question of law to the High Court for a decision.

Of particular relevance to oral hearings are the Inspector's powers to:-

- Take evidence on oath and administer oaths. The same immunities and privileges are available to a person giving evidence as can be claimed by a witness in the High Court, such as self incrimination and solicitor-client confidentiality.

- Require the attendance of a person to give evidence or produce documentation which is relevant. Where such persons refuse to attend they are deemed to be guilty of a criminal offence.

On the closing of the hearing or the completion of his investigations, the Inspector will prepare a report on the appeal, which includes recommendations on a decision. The Board will then determine the appeal in light of this report, although they are not bound to follow it. This report is available to the public for a small cost.

It should be noted regarding costs that the Board can direct the planning authority to pay the appellant's costs irrespective of the outcome of the appeal. However they may also be awarded against the appellant in favour of the authority. Costs in excess of £200 can only be awarded on ministerial sanction.

The Board's Decision

Once An Bord Pleanála has reached its decision the matter is at an end as far as planning considerations go. The only way to take the issue further is through a judicial review, challenging the validity of the Board's decision in the High Court on the grounds of improper procedure or on a matter of law. It will not rehear just the facts of the appeal and change the decision.

THE PLANNING SYSTEM
ENVIRONMENTAL ISSUES

The planning system has seen a number of developments in the area of environmental protection. Just as with the rest of the system, there is plenty of scope for campaign groups to have a say in the process.

Environmental Impact Statements (EIS)

A developing area of the planning process is Environmental Impact Assessment (EIA). Under the legislation certain developments must be accompanied by an Environmental Impact Statement (EIS), showing the expected effects on the environment of the proposed development. This covers most large scale developments, including chemical factories, infrastructural projects, urban development projects and hotels with more than 400 beds. This makes planning applications more complex, with the result that the planning authority has a role at an earlier stage in the process to determine if an EIS is necessary and what it should include.

It is usual, in large projects, for the developer to have extensive pre-application consultations with the planning authority to reach a measure of agreement on what will need to be covered by the planning application and any EIS.

Integrated Pollution Control (IPC) Licensing

Regulations made under the 1992 Environmental Protection Agency Act now provide for a system of Integrated Pollution Control Licensing. Here, one licence is issued to cover all the different aspects of polluting emissions from a particular development. The range of activities within the IPC licensing system has gradually been broadened. Significant industrial, chemical and pharmaceutical activities are covered.

Whereas, in the past, licences or permits were obtained by application to the Local Authority, under the IPC regime, the EPA is the licensing authority. The EPA encourages extensive pre-application consultation with developers and publishes what are known as BATNEEC (Best Available Technology Not Entailing Excessive Costs) guidance notes. These show developers the pollution guidelines which they will have to follow.

The form of application for an IPC licence requires advertisement, both in newspapers and a site notice, to provide third parties with notice of the application and to enable them to make representations to the EPA. The procedures are closely modelled on the planning procedures, described above, in terms of the rights of consultation and representation by third parties who have objections or representations to make in relation to a licence application.

The system differs somewhat in that the EPA, having considered the matter, will issue a draft licence. This draft will be submitted to the applicant, the local Planing Authority and all parties who have made representations. If any party has an objection to the proposed licence, they can make that objection to the EPA who will then handle the matter in a way similar to the way in which An Bord Pleanála handle planning appeals (see above).

Having considered the objections, the EPA will make a final decision on the licence and will issue that decision to all parties and will advertise the fact in a newspaper.

The EPA's decision on a licence application is final and there is no further appeal. The only challenge which can be made is by way of Judicial Review, provided proceedings are brought within two months of the decision.

In addition to the functions outlined above, the EPA must maintain a register of all licences granted, which will be available for inspection by members of the public.

Campaign Strategy

It is important for campaign groups to establish precisely which element of a development is to be the subject of their campaign – is it to be the planning or Environmental Impact Study aspect, by way of representations to the Local Authority or An Bord Pleanála; or is it to be the licensing aspect in relation to emissions to the environment, by way of representations to the EPA in respect of an Integrated Pollution Control licence?

REACHING A CAMPAIGN DECISION

If you think that some form of legal action or involvement in the planning process would help achieve your campaign goals, then start by setting up a sub-group to look into it. In smaller groups this task might be done by an individual or the main committee.

The group's approach to legal matters is very important – if a case is not prepared properly, or a planning appeal is incomplete, no amount of campaign rhetoric can get things back on course. A good legal sub-group should consist of people who are clear thinkers – the organised and meticulous type. Its role would be to investigate the options open to the group, to gather information about the requirements, procedures and costs and to form an opinion on the likelihood of success. This would require taking some legal advice.

Following on from this, the Co-ordinating Committee can make a decision on whether to pursue any form of legal action. Careful consideration needs to be given to a number of elements here. What are the chances of complete or partial success? Can the group afford the financial costs? How tough is the opposition? How long will the process take? Does the group have the energy and commitment required?

While some of the answers may be off-putting at first, if it looks like there is a chance of campaign success through some form of action, then the group should look at ways of overcoming the obstacles. The cost is a big one, but remember that these expenses will be spread out over proceedings, and your fund-raising efforts can be organised to reflect this. Also, you may be lucky and find people who will work for free, or at a reduced rate. Yes, there is an element of risk, but sometimes risks need to be taken to win a campaign.

If the decision is to go ahead, the next step is to get together a legal team. This team will be responsible for information gathering, building up the case, and bringing it through the legal or planning system. It should include whatever legal professionals are required for dealing with a case at the chosen level:-

- **Solicitor** – a lawyer with a general grounding in legal matters. They can represent you themselves in the District Court, but for the higher courts they may wish to engage a barrister on your behalf. The group's usual solicitor, who may have helped with setting up the group, might fill this role.

- **Barrister** – a specialist advocate who can represent your group in the higher courts. Barristers are divided into two groupings, Senior Counsel and Junior Counsel, with Senior Counsel being more experienced and therefore more expensive. Normally you don't deal directly with a barrister, unless at a consultation or around the time of a hearing, as this task falls to your solicitor.

Once this team is up and running, you are in the hands of the professionals.

Good luck!

'YES, YOUR HONOUR!'

It must be remembered that the law cuts both ways, and there are a number of instances where a campaign group, or people within the group, could find themselves hauled before the courts.

Libel and Slander

These two torts, or civil wrongs, are often mixed up.

Basically, libel involves defamation in permanent form, such as in print, whereas slander involves a less permanent form, such as saying something false about a person.

As these are civil wrongs, generally the plaintiff must prove that damages have been suffered as a result of what was said. However, there are a number of exceptions, of which the most relevant to campaign groups might be a statement published maliciously and calculated to affect a person in their trade or profession.

Mere vulgar abuse is not actionable. Saying that someone is a 'right bastard' should not land you in court, which is probably just as well really!

However, even when a person is not referred to directly, if it can be shown that it is obvious whom the words were aimed at, then this can lead to a successful action.

The basis of liability in these situations is very strict, as the law has a strong presumption that everyone is entitled to their reputation. If what was said was actually wrong, it may not be a defence to claim that the person took reasonable care to ensure that what was said was true, or that they honestly believed that they were telling the truth.

It should be clear from this that campaign groups need to be very careful about the truth of any information which they circulate, such as through press releases and newsletters. Landing in court might draw attention to your group, but is likely to detract from your campaign message, as well as damage your credibility – unless of course you win!

Injunctions – The Other Side of the Coin

Some forms of protest, such as blocking access to an office building, might be counteracted by means of an injunction.

Details of the process of getting an injunction have already been covered under Courts Procedure above. However, the implications of being on the receiving end warrant mention as well.

Injunctions limit the protest options available to a group, and are usually used to prevent actions which, though illegal, are likely to be very effective. A second drawback is that if the group breaks the injunction, it brings them into conflict with the courts, not the person who sought the injunction. The consequences can be quite severe, and may involve seizing the group's assets, or even jailing people for contempt of Court. This could also detract from the campaign message, and let the campaign targets keep a low profile.

On the positive side, it is an acknowledgment that your campaign is starting to bite when the opposition has to resort to injunctions. It can also provide publicity, and can be portrayed as a heavy-handed attempt to silence protest while hiding behind the courts.

If your group is on the receiving end of an injunction, study the wording of the order carefully. Get legal advice in order to avoid breaking it unintentionally. Also, remember that this is just one avenue which has been closed off, and you should bring other elements of your strategy to bear with renewed vigour.

Trespass

Entering on private property could also land you in court. Such action would be illegal and would make defendants liable to pay damages.

Make the Best of It!

If you manage to end up in court due to peaceful campaigning, don't let it bother you too much. Use it as another way of focusing attention on your campaign, and the sacrifices people are willing to make in order to achieve its aims.

ANECDOTE: DUBLIN BAY ACTION FOR HEALTH GROUP'S 'NO TO INCINERATION' CAMPAIGN.

The **DBAFHG** *is an umbrella organisation for a number of residents' organisations from Ringsend, Irishtown, Sandymount, Blackrock and Clontarf. It was set up in July 1994 to oppose the application by a local company to build a medical waste incinerator near Ringsend. After a long battle, the group won their campaign when An Bord Pleanála upheld Dublin Corporation's decision to refuse the company planning permission.*

As we wanted to state our case opposing the development before the planning process went too far, we felt it was really important firstly to lobby our political representatives and get them on our side. To win their support and to show them it was a live issue for everyone, we had to get the local people behind us in force through public meetings, rallies and public protests. At the same time, with the help of a local architect, we submitted an objection to Dublin Corporation, along with thousands of signatures.

Some of our politicians organised a meeting for us with the planning officials in the Corporation, and many attended themselves, echoing our views. In the event, Dublin Corporation voted unanimously against the proposed incinerator, and the planners turned it down on a number of grounds – none of them environmental, of course, with the division now between the EPA and the planning authority – a division which made our work much more difficult.

The company appealed the decision to An Bord Pleanála and so did we, as we felt the grounds on which the refusal was based were not as strong as they should have been. Around this time we also managed to arrange a meeting with an official from the Department of Health. It was important for our case to be clear that it was not Department of Health policy to incinerate medical waste.

We took on Tom Menton, a leading environmental solicitor, as we needed to put everything into winning, although we hadn't the money at the time to pay any fees! We also linked up with other environmental groups both here and in England – anyone whose experience and expertise could assist us.

Coming up to the Oral Hearing, it was all about maintaining the pressure, keeping the issue alive in the media, organising public support and on-going lobbying of our politicians. We were very lucky in that Michael McDowell TD and Barrister represented us for free at the Hearing, so that the expertise and professionalism of our case was very evident. Also all our other TDs and many Councillors attended the hearing and made statements in our support.

After the verdict, the final piece of work was organising the celebration!

Geraldine Murphy, Spokesperson

'Ah well, many books. Of the making of books there is no end. I will close by reminding myself and others that writing, reading, thinking are of value only when combined with effective action.'

Edward Abbey,
Environmental author and activist.

APPENDIX A
POLITICAL STRUCTURES

LOCAL AUTHORITY/ COUNCILLORS

The elected Local Authorities are the County Councils (29), County Borough Corporations (5), Borough Corporations (5), Urban District Councils (49) and boards of town commissioners (30). The following services are provided by all County Councils and Corporations with the Urban District Councils and Town Commissioners playing a reduced role.

- Housing and Building;
- Road Transportation and Safety;
- Water Supply and Sewerage;
- Development Incentives and Controls;
- Environmental Protection;
- Recreation and Amenities;
- Agriculture, Education, Health and Welfare;
- Miscellaneous Services.

County Councils have from 20 to 46 members, County Borough Councils have from 15 to 52, Borough Councils 12, UDCs and Boards of Town Commissioners have 9 members.

Local elections are held about every four years. The elected representatives do not receive a salary, but are paid attendance and other allowances. Most have other full or part-time jobs which provide their basic income. Quite a few County or City Councillors are also TDs or Senators with the majority being members of political parties.

Local Authority service provides a useful training ground and a stepping stone into the Dáil or Seanad. It is also seen as a way of keeping in touch with constituents, and maintaining the flow of information and 'favours' essential to the political process.

Full-time Officers and Managers are employed to advise the Councillors and, with the help of their staff, to implement agreed policies. While most of the practical work of the Authority is carried out by these employees, ultimate responsibility for decision-making is vested in the elected representatives. However, unofficially, the power of the Officers can also be substantial.

The administration of the Authority's work is split up into a number of Departments, while overall policy is decided by Council Committees. Some Committees are only able to make recommendations to the Council, while others have delegated powers to decide on behalf of the Council. All decisions of a Local Authority have to fall within its statutory duties and powers.

Council Committee meetings are held in cycles, usually about every four to six weeks, with a meeting of the whole Council at the end of each cycle at which the various Committee decisions are discussed and approved. There tends to be a recess around August, but this varies between authorities. All of the meetings are open to the public, once you are invited by a Councillor.

The Council members have specific Reserved Functions, which involve setting the overall direction for the management of their area. Management are then charged with implementing the Council's decisions, and their role comes under Executive Functions.

The Cathaoirleach is elected by the Council members at the first meeting of the year.

DÁIL/TDs

There are currently 166 deputies in Dáil Éireann. A member is officially called 'Teachta Dála' – 'Deputy to the Dáil' -but is generally known as a TD.

General Elections to the Dáil must be held every four years. The country is split up into 41 constituencies, each of which elects three, four or five TDs. At least one TD must exist for every 20,000 to 30,000 people. Under the Constitution the Government is responsible to the Dáil alone.

It is a TD's job to represent their constituents, thereby providing a democratic channel between the people and Parliament. Their time is divided between the needs of the community, encouraging close links between people and groups in the area, and participating in Dáil sessions and its specialist Committees. Deputies will often also be members of international bodies and of Local Authorities, health boards, VECs and other public bodies. Most TDs hold regular clinics, also known as advice centres, where they meet personally with constituents.

The Dáil normally sits on Tuesdays (14.30 – 21.10), Wednesdays and Thursdays (10.30 – 17.40), so most TDs are in Dublin on those days, and in their constituencies during the rest of the week. The main summer recess occurs in August, but this may change depending on the nature of business. Summer is usually much quieter than the rest of the year, but the committee meetings continue.

There are no hard and fast rules in relation to the yearly schedule. It all depends on what's happening in the country at the time, yet most sittings occur from January to July and October to December.

SEANAD/SENATORS

Within 90 days of the dissolution of Dáil Éireann, a General Election to the Seanad must be held. The 60 Senators to be elected are chosen as follows:-

- 11 are nominated by the Taoiseach.

- 43 are elected by five panels representing vocational interests, namely Culture and Education, Agriculture, Labour, Industry and Commerce, and Public Administration. These panels are made up of members of the incoming Dáil, the outgoing Seanad and Local Authorities.

- 3 are elected by the graduates of the National University of Ireland, and 3 by the graduates of Trinity College, Dublin.

In theory, Seanad Éireann does not recognize party affiliations, but because of the make up of the voting panels and the influence of the Taoiseach, party strengths in the Dáil tend to be reflected.

The Seanad normally meets on Wednesdays (beginning at 14.30) and Thursdays (beginning at 10.30). It often spends time debating important issues, sometimes with greater freedom than the Government as it, unlike the government, is not answerable to the Dáil, and so its fate will not be at stake. The sittings are largely dependent on the amount of business referred from the Dáil.

A Senator is an elected member of Seanad Éireann. In this capacity, they can be involved in initiating new legislation as well as revising proposed legislation, sent from the Dáil before it is due to be implemented.

In more recent times, Senators have a greater voice through the setting up of a system of Joint Committees. These committees include representatives from both houses of the Oireachtas, who would meet, discuss and vote on certain current and topical issues.

Like Deputies, Senators are frequently members of other public bodies. Some also hold local clinics in their constituencies. They make themselves available to offer support, advice and guidance to groups and members of the public on matters relating to State administration.

GOVERNMENT

The Government Cabinet, that is the Taoiseach and Ministers, is the supreme decision-making body in the country. The Taoiseach has the most powerful position, being the person who selects and dismisses Ministers, who appoints Committees and who organises Cabinet re-shuffles. Cabinet's activities, along with those of its many and sometimes secret Cabinet Committees, are carried out behind the public eye.

The Government must have no less than seven and no more than 15 members. Not more than two can be members of the Seanad and the rest, including the Taoiseach, Tánaiste and Minister for Finance, must be members of the Dáil.

While the Government is accountable to the Dáil, Ministers have the right to attend and to be heard in each House. A maximum of 17 Ministers of State can be appointed to assist Government Ministers in their parliamentary and departmental work. The Attorney General is appointed by the Taoiseach, to advise the Government in 'matters of law and legal opinion'.

Cabinet usually meets twice a week in Government Buildings.

THE EUROPEAN UNION/ MEPs

European Commission

The Commission initiates and drafts legislation, oversees its implementation and makes sure that the Treaties are respected. It is basically the civil service of the EU.

It has a five-year mandate, and is composed of two members from each of the larger countries, and one from each of the smaller ones, including Ireland. The Commissioners must be impartial, acting independently from their national Governments, for the common good. Its large staff are mostly based in Brussels in Departments called Directorates General.

Council of Ministers

The Council of Ministers approves directives put forward by the Commission and comprises one Minister from each of the Member States. The Ministers usually carry a similar policy portfolio to that from their home country, such as Health, Finance, Agriculture. The General Affairs Council is attended by all the Foreign Ministers.

Each Member State holds the Presidency of the Council for 6 months on a rota basis. The European Council, comprising the heads of each country and the President of the Commission, meets at least twice a year.

European Parliament

The European Parliament takes part in the legislative process, ratifies most international agreements created by the EU, approves the incoming Commission (which it has the power to dismiss), takes part in the budgetary process, adopts the budget, and calls other institutions to account in public. It primarily acts as a forum for European public opinion, and as the guardian of citizen's rights. It receives petitions, appoints the EU Ombudsman, and allows us a say through our MEPs.

The Parliament presently consists of 629 MEPs, 15 of whom are elected in the Republic of Ireland, and three in Northern Ireland. It is elected every five years. The President is elected for two and a half years and, along with 14 Vice-Presidents, forms the Parliament's Bureau.

APPENDIX B
REFERENCES &
ADDRESSES

REFERENCES

Directory of Libraries and Information Services in Ireland: Produced by the Library Council of Ireland, 53 Upper Mount St., Dublin 2. Approximately £15.

Directory of Irish Archives: Produced by the Irish Academic Press, Blackrock, Co Dublin. Approximately £20.

IPA Diary: Produced by the Institute of Public Administration (IPA), 57-61 Lansdowne Road, Dublin 4. Approximately £39.

Kompass Directory: Produced by Kompass Ireland, Kompass House, Parnell Court, Parnell Square, Dublin 1. Approximately £175.

The Irish Funding Handbook: Produced by Creative Activity for Everyone (CAFE), 23/25 Moss Street, Dublin 2. Approximately £10.

Who Owns Whom: Produced by Dun & Bradstreet International, Holles St., Dublin 2. UK & Ireland volume is approximately £400.

ADDRESSES

Combat Poverty Agency, The Bridgewater Centre, Coyngham Road, Dublin 8. Tel: (01) 6706746. Fax: (01) 6706760.

National Social Services Board, 7th Floor, Hume House, Ballsbridge, Dublin 4. Tel: (01) 6059000. Fax: (01) 6059099.

APSO, 29-30 Fitzwilliam Square, Dublin 2. Tel:(01) 6614411. Fax: (01) 6614202.

Trócaire, 169 Booterstown Avenue, Blackrock, Co Dublin. Tel: (01) 2885385. Fax: (01) 2883577.

ENFO, 17, St. Andrew's St., Dublin 2. Tel: (01) 6793144. Fax: (01) 6795204.

European Commission, Irish Office, Jean Monnet Centre, 39

Molesworth St., Dublin 2. Tel: (01) 6712244 Fax: (01) 6712657.
European Parliament, Irish Office, Jean Monnet Centre, 43 Molesworth St., Dublin 2. Tel: (01) 6719100 Fax: (01) 6795391.
Government Information Services, Taoiseach's Department, Upper Merrion Street, Dublin 2. Tel: (01) 6624422. Fax: (01) 6763419.
Government Publications Office, 4-5 Harcourt Road, Dublin 2. Tel: (01) 6613111. Fax: (01) 4752760.
Public Relations Office, Dáil and Seanad, Leinster House, Kildare Street, Dublin 1. Tel: (01) 6789911 ext. 3166/3066. Fax: (01) 6790424.

WORKING MOTHERS

Patricia O'Reilly

'No matter how focused you are on your career, when you've children, you've to adapt' (Jo, market researcher)

'As female high-flyers, we're doomed to be torn between the demands of work and family' (Lorna, marketing)

What sort of careers are best suited to mothers? What's it like being pregnant at work? What maternity leave are you entitled to? Who's going to mind the baby when you return to work? Does this mean the end of your social life? What if you take time at home to rear your family? How will you get back into the workplace?

Working Mothers provides the answers to the questions women are asking today. It also anticipates those they will be asking in years to come. It is for mothers of all ages — single or married, working through choice or of necessity. An informative and entertaining read, it includes plenty of case histories of couples and singles with children ranging from babes in arms to partying teenagers. Also included is a directory of useful contacts and addresses.

A must for every woman trying to balance motherhood with a career outside the home, and for every woman considering it.

A must for every woman trying to balance motherhood with working outside the home, and for every woman considering it.

Patricia O'Reilly is the author of several books including *Dying with Love* (1992) and *Earning Your Living from Home* (1996). She is a writer, researcher and lecturer/trainer.

ISBN 0-86327-583-4

IRISH GUIDE TO COMPLEMENTARY & ALTERNATIVE THERAPIES

Lucy Costigan

This comprehensive handbook provides information on thirty-five alternative and complementary therapies, from aromatherapy and acupuncture through herbalism and homoeopathy to reflexology and reiki. Each entry comprises an introduction to the therapy, benefits of the therapy, case studies, details of training and a list of practitioners in Ireland. Several lesser-known therapies are also briefly described. In the 90s, many people are becoming aware that alternative therapies can offer a safe and effective approach to healing, succeeding where conventional medicine has failed, or curing without the side-effects often encountered with many of today's drugs. *The Guide to Complementary & Alternative Therapies* will provide an invaluable resource for beginners interested in finding out their options as well as practitioners and those working in the health industry.

Lucy Costigan has a long association with the areas of psychotherapy and complementary therapies. She is a member of the Institute for Reality Therapy in Ireland, the Irish Association of Hypno-analysts, and the National Federation of Spiritual Healers.

ISBN 0-86327-584-2

*Available from bookshops
or direct from*
WOLFHOUND PRESS
*68 Mountjoy Square,
Dublin 1
Tel: (01) 8740354*